CONNECTING INNER POWER WITH GLOBAL CHANGE

CONNECTING INNER POWER WITH GLOBAL CHANGE

The Fractal Ladder

PRAVIR MALIK

Response
Business books from SAGE
Los Angeles ▪ London ▪ New Delhi ▪ Singapore ▪ Washington DC
www.sagepublications.com

First published in 2009 by

Response Books
Business books from SAGE
B1/I-1, Mohan Cooperative Industrial Area
Mathura Road, New Delhi 110 044, India

SAGE Publications Inc
2455 Teller Road
Thousand Oaks
California 91320, USA

SAGE Publications Ltd
1 Oliver's Yard, 55 City Road
London EC1Y 1SP, United Kingdom

SAGE Publications Asia-Pacific Pte Ltd
33 Pekin Street
#02-01 Far East Square
Singapore 048763

Published by Vivek Mehra for Response Books, typeset in 12/14 pt Berkeley by Innovative Processors, Delhi and printed at Chaman Enterprises, New Delhi.

Library of Congress Cataloging-in-Publication Data

Malik, Pravir.
  Connecting inner power with global change: the fractal ladder/Pravir Malik.
    p. cm.
  Includes bibliographical references.
  1. Organizational sociology. 2. Organizational change. 3. Social change. I. Title.

HM786.M32   302.3'5—dc22   2009   2009029792

ISBN: 978-81-321-0221-2 (PB)

The SAGE Team: Reema Singhal, Pranab Jyoti Sarma and Trinankur Banerjee

*This book is dedicated to those heroes through all time
who through the exercise of inner power
have brought about global change*

Contents

List of Figures

Acknowledgements

Through the last two decades I have read a magnificent poem by Sri Aurobindo titled *Savitri*, several times. In the first book of this poem, "The Book of Beginnings," a great yogi, Aswapati, overcomes all terrestrial and cosmic bonds after which, being free, he is able to travel anywhere in creation. The second book "The Book of the Traveler of the Worlds," describes Aswapati's travels, which begins with his perceiving "The World Stair." This particular canto had a deep impact on me. I do not know for sure what the author intends with that canto, but my interpretation of it created a seed with which I began to view many different events around me, and which has resulted in this book. Following are the lines from this canto:

> ... Amid the many systems of the One
> Made by an interpreting creative joy
> Alone it points us to our journey back
> Out of our long self-loss in Nature's deeps;
> Planted on earth it holds in it all realms:
> It is a brief compendium of the Vast.
> This was the single stair to being's goal.
> A summary of the stages of the spirit,
> Its copy of the cosmic hierarchies
> Refashioned in our secret air of self

A subtle pattern of the universe.

It is within, below, without, above.

Acting upon this visible Nature's scheme

It wakens our earth-matter's heavy doze

To think and feel and to react to joy;

It models in us our diviner parts,

Lifts mortal mind into a greater air,

Makes yearn this life of flesh to intangible aims,

Links the body's death with immortality's call:

Out of the swoon of the Inconscience

It labours towards a superconscient Light.

If earth were all and this were not in her,

Thought could not be nor life-delight's response:

Only material forms could then be her guests

Driven by an inanimate world-force.

Earth by this golden superfluity

Bore thinking man and more than man shall bear;

This higher scheme of being is our cause

And holds the key to our ascending fate;

It calls out of our dense mortality

The conscious spirit nursed in Matter's house.

The living symbol of these conscious planes,

Its influences and godheads of the unseen,

Its unthought logic of Reality's acts

Arisen from the unspoken truth in things,

Have fixed our inner life's slow-scaled degrees.

Its steps are paces of the soul's return

From the deep adventure of material birth,

A ladder of delivering ascent

And rungs that Nature climbs to deity…(Sri Aurobindo 1950–51)

Particularly the lines "… A subtle pattern of the universe. It is within, below, without, above …" meant to me that being within, below, without, above, is in effect being everywhere, and perforce on different scale, it could be interpreted as being a fractal. In this interpretation, the fractal consists of physical worlds, vital worlds, and mental worlds stacked one on top of the other, and form part of the blueprint for all existence. While this canto has been written from a Seer's perspective and therefore perhaps cannot even rightly be clearly understood unless one enters into the consciousness of the Seer, this book, by contrast, has been constructed primarily through observation and logic, using reason, applied across time. Hence, the book represents a very different perspective to try to arrive at, through logic, what is evident to a Seer.

"The World Stair" and other cantos in *Savitri* have been the central inspiration for this book, and I remain ever grateful to the poet.

Other life experiences, particularly in working as a consultant to many global corporations has provided insight into business operations and to the self-imposed shackles of mediocrity that bind so many of us to a life of compromise. In particular, through my work at ZS Associates, Ernst & Young, EDS, A.T. Kearney, The Concours Group, Conner Partners, and Business for Social Responsibility, each of which has a different value proposition and quite different operating cultures, I have been able to intersect with large businesses on different fronts and in different ways. To these set of life-experiences and to the consulting organizations that allowed me to experience these, I remain thankful.

There have also been several individuals who knowingly through direct help or unknowingly through extremely confrontational relationships have helped me to learn a lot about my self. To the hand of Progress behind both these groups of people, and to these people themselves, I remain thankful.

There are also several groups of people who have helped make this book a reality. First, I mention a colleague, Professor Sanjay Mukherjee, at the Indian Institute of Management (IIM) Calcutta, who, through the years, has readily accepted several articles that I have written on this subject in the *Journal of Human Values* of which he is the Editor, and who introduced me to Dr Sugata Ghosh, Vice President, Commissioning, SAGE Publications. From the start Dr Ghosh has offered me great support and encouragement for this book. Reema Singhal, Assistant Commissioning Editor at SAGE, had been given the unenviable task of helping make the initial manuscript far easier to read, and her very useful suggestions through the course of the last few months have been instrumental in this regard. Pranab Sarma, Assistant Production Editor, has been given the responsibility of bringing this book into production. Many others from SAGE have helped behind the scenes. This book would not be possible without their help.

Some others have helped through the years with making the overall idea more real. Jugal Kishore Mukherjee, the Head of Knowledge, the undergraduate arm at Sri Aurobindo International Center of Education, where I taught a three-year Flowering of Management course, one day mentioned to me in passing that what I was attempting to do was very difficult—to build a meta-theory about organization. I had never thought of the work with fractals and organizations in that manner, but once he mentioned it, I felt a pressure to do just that. While I had many students at Knowledge, I mention three in particular, Devdip Ganguly, Parashmani Chandra, and Sukrit Dhandhania, whose curiosity and enthusiasm always pushed me to discover more on the overall subject. At about the same time, I also approached Parimala, Editor at *Hindu Business Line,* with a proposal to write a series of articles relating fractals with organizations.

She liked the idea, and with her help and suggestions to alter the writing style for a business audience, a series of seven articles appeared in *Hindu Business Line* within a year. This too gave the work quite a boost.

I also mention R.Y. Deshpande, who is well versed in the works of Sri Aurobindo, and has through the years been a mentor to me in my endeavor to understand more of Sri Aurobindo's works. He and another friend of mine, Debashish Banerjee, have reviewed some of the materials in this book and provided useful suggestions that have helped refine this book. Daryl Conner, another mentor, and Chairman of Conner Partners, a strategy execution consulting company, provided me with guidance on writing a book, based on his own personal experience of writing several books. Last but not the least, I am thankful for the support of Chitvan, my wife, and my two sons, Chaitanya and Aditya, who remained remarkably quiet every Saturday when I would sit down to write this book.

Connecting Inner Power with Global Change: The Fractal Ladder is my third book. As I look back on the contents of the previous two books, I realize how much my thought has changed over the years. Yet at that time those books seemed to represent a summit of personal thought and from my small perspective, timeless. My hope is that years from now, I will come back to this book with the same realization, for then I know that I will not have been seized by stagnation however alluring, and will truly have become a disciple of Progress in my own adventuring through the fractal journeys that define my life now.

To this constant and promising march of Progress I remain ever grateful.

Introduction

The power to change things lies within us. Presented here is a theory on how shifts in oneself can have profound shifts in corporations, markets, systems, and the world. It has been said: "Become the change you wish to see in the World." But the elaboration of how this is true may remain a mystery. The theory of organization introduced here indicates a fractal reality in which an idea, a person, a team, a corporation, a market, a system, progressively more complex constructs, are concretely connected by virtue of common and linked patterns that animates each of these separate levels. Hence, the power to positively change progressively more complex and, in many cases, removed arenas of life, such as climate change, by making corresponding changes in one's personal space, becomes more real.

Such a relationship connecting the micro to the macro has thus far been applied only in the physical realm. Benoît Mandelbrot and others have studied how Nature employs fractal patterns to build complex structures. The fractal theory introduced here indicates how far more complex constructs—such as persons, corporations, markets, countries—comprising significant behavioral components, can similarly be holistically perceived and correspondingly shifted. As a result, a more effective shaping power is put in the hands of those who are able to live the theory.

On many different fronts the world is beginning to experience accelerated crises. Recent times have borne witness to the increasing global financial crises which continues to grow in scope everyday. Not only are more economies pronouncing recessions and tottering on the verge of depression, not only are an increasing number of companies and even diverse financial institutions declaring bankruptcy, but more so, people are continuing to be affirmed and reaffirmed as mere assets or liabilities to be dealt with accordingly. The threat of climate change, increasing resource shortages, and now food security is continuing to grow in intensity. Destruction of natural capital continues at a fiendish pace through inadvertent or even advertent destruction of species, transportation of species from one region of the world to others not suited for such implantation, and release of a constant stream of toxins from an increasing number of sources. As a human species we have often forgotten our routes to freedom and stand enslaved at multiple levels by a formidable global machinery that promises utopia at every step, but, in reality, is set on a path towards its own destruction. One may look at these and other current crises as disconnected. To do so, however, is part of the problem.

This book posits a single system that connects different organizational entities together in a fractal structure. The term "organization" refers to an idea, a habit, a person, a corporation, a collectivity, a country, and even planet earth, amongst other possible entities whose structure, processes, and meaning is defined by architectures comprised of similar building-blocks. An underlying dynamic of this system is posited to be its fractal reality, that is, the ability of an organization to replicate its raison d'être and way of being not only at its own level of operation, but also through influence, on a different scale. Myriad fractal effects emanating from many different sources create a general fractal vortex. This vortex often blinds organizations to high ideals and liberating possibilities, and binds them to habits and norms of yesterday. Within this fractal vortex, however, there exists a remarkable ladder, the Fractal Ladder, a special zone that releases and connects inner power to global change. This Fractal Ladder is constructed by a common fractal for progress that animates each of its rungs. It is at once a mechanism by which the system can progress meaningfully, and acts as a doorway into the heart of the system which is seen as purposeful, conscious, and progressive. The heart of the system manifests itself in building-blocks and organizations. When these organizations embark on a particular fractal journey, the one that spells progress on each rung of the ladder, they can progressively uncover and embody more of the truth of which they are in the final analyses-evolving projections.

Stepping onto this Fractal Ladder is the secret of bringing about meaningful and sustainable global change. The ensuing change is not so much a result of personal effort, though this is certainly indispensable, and the means by which an organization steps onto the Fractal Ladder, but more so because on the Fractal Ladder, the progressive dynamics that lie at the heart of the containing system begin to find expression in better prepared organizations more easily and hence magnify. Deep motive forces that have the power to bring to surface true identity are then released, and organizations begin to develop along a more stable multi-dimensional foundation as opposed to the current travesty of a one-dimensional foundation.

When linearity and simple cause–effect models are the dictionaries by which we ascribe meaning and purpose to our lives, the inaccuracy and resulting action in that view cannot but cause us to encounter formidable obstacles at every step of the way. These then manifest as the many larger-than-life problems that we are faced with today. When we are able to embrace the Fractal Ladder-based systems-view of reality, however, we not only give way to, but also begin to enter into relationship with a more conscious and comprehensive cause–effect reality that necessarily works a greater degree of magic in our lives.

The first half of the book examines dynamics at various levels of organization to extrapolate the existence of a Fractal Ladder which is positioned to be the signature of a progressive, conscious, and fully integrated world-system. Chapter 1 introduces the basic building-blocks of organizations and the pattern that is the basis of the ubiquitous fractal at the base of the Fractal Ladder. Chapter 2 examines the same building-blocks and pattern as it manifests at the level of the person. Chapters 3, 4, and 5 examine the building-blocks and pattern as it manifests at the levels of the business, the economy, and in many system instances, respectively. Each of these chapters explores varied creations that manifest depending on how the building-blocks are combined with one another. There is only one particular combination of the building-blocks, however, that results in progressive and sustainable organizations, and this is posited to be the base-pattern or seed-fractal representative of the Fractal Ladder. Chapter 6 takes a step beyond all human-based creations to examine the very canvas of nature to similarly establish the fact if the base-pattern of the ubiquitous fractal exists there. Chapter 7 takes a step back from the various fields of observation to illustrate the presence of a fantastic ubiquitous fractal—the Fractal Ladder—that in effect links together the similar pattern of progress across the different scales of reality. Further, the Fractal Ladder is posited as part of the signature of a conscious design or implicit aspiration behind things.

The second half of the book begins to explore the different properties, dynamics, and implications of operating in such an integrated, Fractal Ladder-based world-system. In other words, it begins to construct and ascribe alternative meaning and purpose to action and behavior. Such a reconstruction is critical to successful operation in a world that in reality is vastly different from what we imagine. Learning the strokes that allow us to effectively move through this very different medium causes us to remain afloat and even thrive, rather than gasp for breath and sink, as we seem to be doing. Chapter 8, hence, examines many properties in this single world-system. These are positioned as tools and devices by which to begin to maneuver through this very different world. Examination of the Fractal Ladder and related properties begins to reveal the existence of a conscious entity, Progress, which is hypothesized as being the context for the world-system. Chapter 9 takes a deeper dive into the nature of Progress, the heart of the world-system, to further understand how it interacts with and even shapes the Fractal Ladder. Armed now with a clearer understanding of the world-system, the subsequent chapters begin to explore the implications of this new knowledge. Chapter 10, thus, explores what the business and corporation may become as life on the Fractal Ladder continues to progress. The possibility of enlightened reconstruction of basic and pervasive institutions, such as business, that define our modern world depends on the nature of exercised leadership in the scheme of things. Chapter 11 seeks to examine the criticality and nature of such leadership in the future scheme of things. Chapter 12 takes a look at the range of possible futures that may manifest depending on which fundamental building-block or part of the ubiquitous pattern becomes active in the consciousness of people. Chapter 13 examines the transformation that needs to take place in many popular institutions for the best possible future to emerge.

This book puts forward nothing less than a sea-change in the definition and dynamics of many common components of our lives. Our notion of self, world, leadership, progress, money, business, society, and myriad other institutions needs to be turned on its head, not out of any frivolity, but based on more penetrating observations of progress and stagnation that animate many practical aspects of our lives. The contradictions that abound in our life arise because there is a huge disconnect between the common meanings and purposes we ascribe to key components of our life and the meaning and purpose that the truth of our reality demands. The fractal system presented here is an attempt to mirror that truth of our reality more fully.

The approach to achieving effective change naturally changes. Usually the approach to bringing about change is restricted to one or the other level. There are frameworks that deal with making personal changes. There are frameworks that deal with making organizational change. There are frameworks that deal with making market or system changes. These no doubt have their place and utility in the scheme of things, and will assist various organizations to complete their respective fractal journeys as we will discover in this book. The demand placed before us by world circumstances themselves, however, cannot be addressed by such piecemeal and disconnected approaches any longer. The time has come for a radical reconstruction of the notion of drivers, motive forces, causality, and the very map and way of change. This alternative approach to change that integrates the micro with the macro, that gets into deeper subjective drivers and their objective effects, that considers all events, ideas, circumstances, not to mention people, teams, corporations, collectivities, countries—instances of organization—as being constructed and, therefore, even reconstructed by common building blocks, in effect an approach that connects inner power with global change, is what is presented here.

Many new postulates for change emerge in this book. These include the following notions:

- There are common building-blocks that animate each level of organization.
- Organization refers to an idea, a theory, a habit, an event, a circumstance, a person, a team, a corporation, a collectivity, a market, an economy, our world; basically anything whose structure, processes, meaning is defined by the common building-blocks.
- Dynamics of a particular organization are entirely determined by which of these building-blocks are active at that level of organization.
- Like DNA, the stringing together of building-blocks in a particular sequence or with particular dominance, determines the active dynamics of that level of organization.
- There is only one particular sequence of stringing together building-blocks that allows an organization to progress sustainably.
- This particular sequence exists in all progressive organizations, regardless of the level of complexity and forms the seed-pattern of which the Fractal Ladder is the fractal.
- When organizations embrace sequences other than that of the progressive fractal, they become a part of a general fractal vortex that animates ordinary or "as-usual" as opposed to progressive life.
- All sequences tend to repeat their raison d'être and way of being not only at their own levels, but by influence at other levels also. This is what reinforces fractal reality.
- When a fractal for progress inevitably encounters forces or contrary fractals, a rite of passage is created by which deeper identity can emerge.

- The Fractal Ladder is a zone of possibility that causes the world-system to progress in the most sustainable way possible.
- The Fractal Ladder is the signature of a progressive, conscious, and fully integrated world-system.
- The existence of the fractal of progress, regardless of the level of organizational complexity and formidable opposition by forces to the contrary, implies its reality or even an essential and pervasive reality of power, presence, knowledge, and love.
- An opening to this essential reality of power, presence, knowledge, and love is perhaps the most effective way for an organization to complete its own fractal journey of progress.
- The existence of a Fractal Ladder and a personified Progress sets the stage for a vastly different set of dynamics with which one brings about change in organizations.

On many different fronts we are today at a boundary condition. The journey between one phase or building-block of the ubiquitous fractal and the next must be completed for the increasing contradictions and general debilitation along many different fronts, symptoms of a bygone way of being, to decline. Just as in the case of addressing climate change, the window for making this transition is time-bound and those organizations that are able to make this journey demanded of them now, are the ones that will emerge as leaders of our collective future.

CHAPTER OUTLINE

Chapter 1—The Pattern: An introduction to the building-blocks and the pattern that is the basis of the "ubiquitous fractal."

Key Concepts: Dichotomies of life | Life as a vast, interconnected system | Problems caused by lack of systems view | The fractal nature of the system | Why problems can persist | Efforts required to alter the base-pattern | Pattern should be self-evident and pervasive | Beyond geography and history: earth–sun dance | Phases of a day | Physical | Vital | Mental | DNA of the earth | Building-blocks | Formation of kernel | Nature of kernels | Isolated development of kernels | The base or ubiquitous pattern | Complete journey and emergence of identity | Incomplete journey | Triplicity and its bias | Fractal opposition | Rite of passage | Mentality and identity | Evolution of the earth.

Chapter 2—The Person Pattern: A look at the building-blocks and pattern as it manifests at the level of the person.

Key Concepts: Application of fractal architecture in definition of a person | Kernel reality through fractal pressure | Creation of tendencies | Perpetuating the nature of the world | Countering of world's natural commerce with its creatures | Progression through sun-marked fractal and identity | Tendency versus identity | Tendency fractal contrary to ubiquitous fractal | Progressive organization and mentality | Importance of questioning | Uniqueness working itself out through play of tendencies | Living one's uniqueness | Life pattern and Maslow's psychology | Expression of earth through physical, vital, mental masks | Earth becoming an earth–sun | Uniqueness as a creative force.

Chapter 3—The Business Pattern: A look at the building-blocks and pattern as it manifests in business.

Key Concepts: Application of fractal architecture in definition of business | Three types of assets in physical orientation | Three types of flows in vital orientation | Three types of outlooks in mental orientation | Physically-led organization | Vitally-led organization | Mentally-led organization |

Combinations and governance | Kernels or seed-states and fractal pressure | Alignment of kernels with sun-marked physical–vital–mental fractal | Opportunities for "rite of passage" multiplied | Stepping into a particular kernel at will | Fractal link between personal and business levels | Relationship of identity with sun-like properties | Stringing of states and milieu of progress | Strengths and shortcomings of physical, vital, mental orientations | Business logic of integrating three orientations | Automaticity of sun-marked physical–vital–mental fractal at business level | Shift in feeling and thought orientations in bringing about change | Validation of fractal model.

Chapter 4—The Economy Pattern: A look at how this pattern has almost as if automatically appeared at the level of the economy, and how certain parts of the pattern are associated with higher degrees of freedom.

Key Concepts: Bottom-up fractal analysis | Top-down fractal analysis | Global economy fractal | Multiplication of mediocrity | Agriculture and physical phase | Industrial economy and vital phase | Digital economy and mental phase | Automaticity of traversing physical, vital, and mental phases | DNA of life and sun-marked physical–vital–mental fractal | Assessment of progress from physical, vital, and mental points of view | Fractal within a fractal | Approaching limits of the vital phase | Global indicators of a breakdown | Birth of the corporation and fractal pressure | Corporation as a quintessential vital animal | Necessity of completion of sun-marked physical–vital–mental journey for corporation | Sub-phase within a phase | Rite of passage at the economy level | Degrees of freedom | Primary actors of a phase | The vital milieu | Pushing instant gratification to its limits | DNA of life and push to transcend limits | Kernels of chief actors | Tendencies and fractal pressure | Aura of impersonality | Difficulty of change at impersonal levels of organization |

Encountering and surpassing demons of creation | Global economy fractal as expression of individual way of being | Key to global economy shift lies in shift at the individual level.

Chapter 5—The System Pattern: A look at how this pattern has spontaneously emerged across several different disciplines—physics, management thought, biotechnology, amongst others.

Key Concepts: Mental sub-phase of vital phase of global economy | Digital economy fractal | Brochure-ware and the physical-phase | e-Commerce and the vital phase | Re-conceptualization and the mental phase | Increase in degrees of freedom | Energy industry fractal | Oil and gas extraction and physical phase | Maximizing energy flow and vital phase | Alternative energy and mental phase | Global politics fractal | Fractal within a fractal | World War I and II and physical phase | Cold War and vital phase | Globalization and mental phase | Exchange rate fractal | Gold standard and physical phase | Balance of power and vital phase | Real-time creativity and mental phase | Science-based systems of thought | Physics fractal | Atomic view and physical phase | Quantum view and vital phase | Unifying theme and mental phase | Biomimicry fractal | Form and function and physical phase | Imitation of process and vital phase | Whole systems view and mental phase | Organizational design fractal | Silo-mentality and physical phase | Process view and vital phase | Raison d'être and mental phase | Fractal for progress | Element-focus and physical phase | Experimentation and vital phase | Mastery and mental phase | Leaders push the sequence | Sun-marked physical–vital–mental fractal in DNA of life as causal agent of progress.

Chapter 6—The Evolution Pattern: A look at evolution of life on earth, and how the patterns that are emerging in different fields of life parallels this overarching or base pattern.

Key Concepts: Nature of creation as function of sequencing of building-blocks | Single ladder | Blue-print of progress | The evolution fractal | Records of evolution and progressive manifestation | Physical sub-phase of physical phase of evolution fractal | Atomic particles and physical sub–sub-phase | Fusing together and vital sub–sub-phase | Identity of form and mental sub–sub-phase | Closed-system interaction and vital sub-phase of physical phase of evolution fractal | Yearning and mental sub-phase of physical phase | Autonomous cellular activity at physical sub-phase of vital phase of evolution fractal | Experimentation and vital sub-phase of vital phase of evolution fractal | Increased yearning for identity and mental sub-phase of vital phase of evolution fractal | Culmination of vital phase of evolution fractal and basis of mental phase of evolution fractal | Simple thought elements and physical sub-phase in mental phase of evolution fractal | Choice and experimentation and vital sub-phase in mental phase in evolution fractal | Advanced mind-elements and mental sub-phase of mental phase of evolution fractal | "What the eye can see" and physical sub–sub-phase of mental sub-phase of mental phase of evolution fractal | Beginnings of history | Vital sub–sub-phase of mental sub-phase of mental phase of evolution fractal | Transition from vital sub–sub-phase to mental sub–sub-phase of mental phase of evolution fractal | Recorded history as journey through vital sub–sub-phase | Birth of Internet as a water-shed event | Internet soft-voice fractal | Beginning of open communication and physical phase of Internet soft-voice fractal | Multiplication of voices and vital phase of soft-voice fractal | Shifting of power and mental phase of soft-voice fractal | Carbon-based economy as surfacing of embedded physical–vital patterns | Carbon-based economy as a rite of passage | Earth–sun dance | Extending the Gaia hypothesis: Earth becomes an earth–sun | Fractal architecture applied to earth–sun dance | Astronomy and the physical view of the earth–sun dance |

Astrology and vital view of earth–sun dance | Purpose and meaning and mental view of earth–sun dance | Sun-potential.

Chapter 7—The Fractal Ladder: The linking together of the similar patterns appearing across different fields and systems, in reality different "scales," to illustrate a fantastic ubiquitous fractal—perhaps part of a signature of a conscious design or implicit aspiration behind things.

Key Concepts: Pathways | Common building-blocks | Extending idea of fractal geometry into complex behavioral structures | World out there is not really a world out there | Fractal reality versus Fractal Ladder | Fractal Ladder as a way out of contradictions | Key to climbing the Fractal Ladder | Story of progress and the physical–vital–mental journey | Climbing the rungs of the Fractal Ladder to connect inner power to global change | Step-wise journey | The Fractal Ladder as a fractal for progress | The miracle of progress | Upward and downward causality | Universality of downward causality | Safe passage in the vortex | Personification of Progress | Progress as a witness | Creation, power, and change in the world | Qualities of Progress: omnipresence, omniscience, omnipotence, omnicaring | Progress as a Mother | Relationship with Progress | Exceptional beings | Secret of power | Progress and stagnated journeying | Shifting our story of disbelief by completing the sun-marked physical–vital–mental journey | Our tremendous choice.

Chapter 8—Fractal Properties: Examination of properties in a fractal world. These become tools, devices by which to maneuver through a very different world.

Key Concepts: Application of fractal lens to better exercise our power in the world | Fractal model as an elaborate systems-view of the world | Progressive state and system evolution | Arranging properties by the triple view | Fractal Ladder seed-pattern | Physical properties to do with structure | Fractal universality | Universality connecting various fields | From a linear to a systems view | Fractal influence | Influence as giving the Fractal Ladder its ladder-like quality | Threshold of influence | Magnification caused by fractal influence | Fractal recursion | Recursion as applying fractal to sub-phase of journey | Recursive property used to piece together likely development of entities | Recursive property used to shed light on structure of entities | Fractal completion | Tendency of fractal to want to complete its journey | Fractal step-wise development | Capabilities of former phases increasing leverage of subsequent phases | Fractal evolution | Evolution alters conditions within which base journey exists | Spiral nature of journey on the Fractal Ladder | Fractal matrixing | Matrixing as a devise to perpetuate progress by leveraging established insights into progress | Vital properties to do with process | Fractal intersection | Intersection of fractals potentially causes each to progress | Religion fractal | Reviewing world conflicts through the lens of fractal influence | Fractal facilitation | Facilitation of stagnation by application of physical–vital–mental fractal | Status quo–chaos–questioning | Fractal flow | Flow as a property by which a range of energies enter into a situation | Fractal upscaling | Upscaling implies shifting from a disconnected linear to a one-system view | Mental properties to do with meaning | World-wiseliness | The more physical–vital–mental journeys one masters the more world-wisely one becomes | World-wiseliness and convergence and prevalence of fractals | Mirroring | All is a reflection of an inner state | Nothing lies on the Fractal Ladder | Affirmation | Successful outcome in the world as a result of the physical–vital–mental journey | Integration | Integration of physical, vital, mental, and underlying purpose | Integration and leadership | Uniqueness | Uniqueness as an outcome of the fractal journey | A fourth class of properties | Alignment with sense of progress | Aspiration for progress |

Surrender of difficulties and dilemmas | Rejection of contrary fractals | Love for an omnicaring entity.

Chapter 9—The Nature of Progress: Examination of the nature of progress and how that interacts with and ultimately shapes the Fractal Ladder.

Key Concepts: The initial state | Creation has proceeded under the aegis of Progress | Reviewing manifested creation in understanding properties of Progress | Insight into transitions and trajectories when properties understood | Sequence to progress yielding to a fourth state | Insight into seed-state providing guidance in selecting emerging pathways | Who we become determined by nature of Progress | All-presence of Progress | All-knowingness of Progress | All-power of Progress | All-caringness of Progress | Properties co-exist and act in simultaneity in management of Fractal Ladder | Top-down versus bottom-up analysis of properties | Manifested states or physical, vital, mental building-blocks tell us something about Progress | "Perfection" and "service" at the physical level | Parallels between the top-down and bottom-up observations | All-presence and the physical state | Limitations of properties of Progress in nature | Power of energy versus light of energy | Adventure as proceeding under the aegis of power | All-power and the vital state | "Adventure," "energy," "assertiveness," "growth" as characteristics of all-power | Questioning and the heart of knowledge | All-knowingness and the mental state | Impersonal and personal qualities of Progress | Omnicaring and heart | The fourth state— intuition | Intuition as a border-state connecting the top-down with the bottom-up | Rule of Heart | Fragmented creations of manifested nature | Physical, vital, mental states as fields of possibility | Changing action of properties of Progress in different fields of possibility | Fixed grooves of the physical | Physical–vital conglomerate | Uniqueness and identity manifest at the mental level | Intuition and more direct action from nature of Progress | Observed nature | Service as observed nature of property of omnipresence | Adventure as observed nature of property of omnipotence | Knowledge as observed nature of property of omniscience | Harmony as observed nature of property of omnicaring | Application of the physical–vital–mental architecture to Progress | Physical aspect of Progress as physical, vital, mental, intuitional states | Vital aspect of Progress as Service, Adventure, Knowledge, Harmony | Mental aspect of Progress as omnipresence, omnipotence, omniscience, omnicaring | Secret names behind the operation of the Fractal Ladder | Reduction of rigidities in building-blocks through action of intuition | Darker or shadow-states of physical, vital, mental | Structure, process, meaning of Fractal Ladder evolving rapidly | Basis of operation shifting from narrow one-dimensionality to holistic multi-dimensionality | AUM and the Fractal Ladder.

Chapter 10—Remaking the Business World: A look at what business and the corporation may become as the Fractal Ladder continues to progress.

Key Concepts: Comprehension of current problems through examination of related business fractals | Consumerism fractal, business fractal, global economy fractal, global society fractal | Choice of consumption as dictated from the physical, vital, mental ways of being | Wal-Mart and testament to being at the vital level of consumer fractal | Changing the root dynamic to bring about progression of related business fractals | Extent of impact of the root dynamics and the wake-up call | Climate change as essence of the wake-up call | Climate change as the result of a vital way of being | Business fractal at the vital level | Global economy fractal on vital side of boundary between vital and mental | Nature of boundary | Global society fractal and business standards of judgment | Progress of society as synonymous with progress of business | Global society fractal at the vital level | Pervasive vital-centeredness indicating severe loss of balance | Climate change as a rebellion of matter | Individual consciousness as the root of the world fractal | The remaking of business through shift in individual consciousness | The essence of CSR | CSR can give the appearance that a real shift in consciousness has occurred | False solutions and other disequilibrium as severe as climate change | Climate change as a wake-up call to the vital way of being | Nature of transition from the vital to the mental way of being | Different ways to accelerate shift from the vital to mental way of being | Mobilization of secret names of Progress | New creation of business must have four motive forces as foundation | People being allowed to follow their essential way of being as key to new creation | Organizations with enduring power have mobilized something of four motive forces simultaneously | Instability caused by following shadow-state of one motive force only | The great tragedy of current corporate life | Modern business versus grassroots community-driven development | Nature of leadership as the deciding factor.

Chapter 11—Future Leadership: A look at the criticality and importance of leadership in the future scheme of things.

Key Concepts: Puppets and cogs in a machine | Progress requires that particular circumstances be the field of an instrument | An unknowing instrument requires mastery over elements of the physical, vital, and/or mental | Elemental leadership versus holistic leadership | Holistic leadership causes more complete projections from the heart of Progress | Creation of unique personalities of deeper substance | Holistic leadership in tune with Progress is the need of the hour | Restructuring of existing building-blocks to counter past habits | Dynamism as a result of integrating the inner with the outer | Inner power versus physical–vital–mental power | Identity and progressive unfoldment determined by progressive unfoldment of Progress | Bringing uniqueness/ *dharma* to the surface by adoption of more dynamic nature | Defining leadership | Task and necessity of 21st century leadership is redefinition on every level of creation | Living approach that will willingly cause people to change | Altering the symbolic reality of the physical, vital, mental | Deeper drivers have their own power and break held limits | Double-action of motive forces | Simultaneous driver action and tipping the balance toward more progressive development | Creation of inertia of physical | Creation of aggression of vital | Creation of narrowness and impotency of mental | Shifting of personality through action of drivers | Bringing into being a new modus operandi that mirrors essence of Progress | Fractal properties as a means of reinterpretation | From isolationist physical–vital based reality to mental–intuitional fractal-animated systems-based reality | Inevitability of manifestation of *dharmas* | Developing intimacy with Progress.

Chapter 12—Alternative Futures: A look at global realities and how different futures may emerge depending on what part of the fractal pattern becomes active collectively.

Key Concepts: Existence of Progress as indication of direction of development for humanity | "Physical" incarnation of Fractal Ladder | Physical–service–perfection conglomerate | Vital–adventure–courage conglomerate | Mental–knowledge–wisdom conglomerate | Intuitional–harmony–mutuality conglomerate | Alteration of base-fractal of which Fractal Ladder is a creation | "Vital" incarnation of Fractal Ladder | Physical–service–perfection–omnipresence conglomerate | Vital–adventure–courage–omnipotence conglomerate | Mental–knowledge–wisdom–omniscience conglomerate | Intuitional–harmony–mutuality–omnicaring conglomerate | "Mental" incarnation of Fractal Ladder | Possibility and apotheosis present at each moment of space and time | Choices made now determine timing of future incarnations of Fractal Ladder | Alternative paths as alternative futures | Connection and integration at crux of the Fractal Ladder | Fractal Ladder surrounded by general fractal vortex | Realization of reality of fractal-based system implies operation approaching intuitional level | Operation at intuitional level expedites uniqueness | Physical orientation scenario | Nature of catastrophe in physical scenario | Façade dynamics | Vital orientation scenario | Limit dynamics | Impact on psychological health | Loss of subjective power | Causal relationship between subjectivity and objectivity reversed | Asset view of life | Inherent and disproportionate value ascribed to money | Impact on physical health | Impact on global political stability | Lack of idealism and balanced development | Seed-pattern works itself out on a global-scale supply chains as organizations of destruction | Needless and wasteful resource extraction, manufacturing, and consumption | CSR makes no difference unless base consciousness of citizens changes | Mental orientation scenario | The value of questioning | Questioning at different ends of the mental orientation spectrum | Limits of questioning | Creation of more thoughtful though silo'd institutions | Burst of apparent creativity | Intuitional orientation scenario | Developing a witness consciousness | Emergence of uniqueness-based manifestations in various fields | Form follows spirit | Citizens as heroes who act from the core.

Chapter 13—Transformation: A look at the transformation that needs to take place in many popular institutions.

Key Concepts: Shifting from the physical–vital orientation to the mental–intuitional orientation | Worldview needing to be turned on its head | Focusing on the physical only is to miss the context of life | Consigning ourselves to littleness and lack of possibility through a physical–vital orientation | Physical–vital power as one that accelerates the debilitation of the world-system | Condition for meaningful global change | Necessity of sea-change in personal psychology | Co-responsibility as a creative center of a sustainably progressing world-system | Boundary conditions and individual leadership | Logically thought out change versus change resulting form shift in consciousness | Creative stillness in the eye of the fractal storm | Becoming a compelling center for the creation of a new organizational reality | Alternative drivers behind business organization | Business-as-expression-of-uniqueness paradigm | Force and authenticity of motive force incarnations creating natural leaders | Business as a note in a fantastic score orchestrated by Progress | Pauperization of mosaic of commerce by focus on money rather than uniqueness | Sense of money re-contextualized by completion of its own fractal | Shift in context of life in mental–intuitional orientation | Value of money from the physical–vital and mental–intuitional perspectives | Different measurements of worth | Focus on accumulation and financial crises | Fixing attention on underlying progress rather than accumulation of money | Current perception of money as a great binding chain | Physical–vital orientation as one of limitation and high cost of money | Mental–intuitional orientation as one of increasing abundance and low cost of money | A re-contextualized mosaic of commerce | A freer, more possibility-faced mosaic for each institution of society | Mosaic as an expression of a collectivity | The four characteristics and the essence of a country culture | Mental–intuitional orientation allows deeper and formative dynamics to come into being | International relations as a function of mutual learning and exchange of living cultures.

1

The Pattern

A SINGLE HUMAN–EARTH SYSTEM

It has been said that we are all authors of our own lives, and depending on the attitude, perceptions, and thoughts that form the kernel of our being, we create realities that resonate with that kernel. As we look at the contemporary unfolding of life around us, we cannot but at first sight be struck by the juxtaposition of vast contraries. On the one hand, there is the beauty of nature reflected in star and sun, tree, bird, and cloud, amongst her many constructs. On the other, man's progressive despoliation of it, apparent in the thoughtless extraction of nature's resources, and the often equally thoughtless constructs whether of steel, cement, or the myriad other compositions ranging from cosmetics to elaborate electronics resulting from incompletely conceived designs. On the one hand there is the glint in the eye that hints at the implicit creativity, power, love, and possibility resident in each living being, and on the other the continued exploitation, compression, slavery, killing of all that possibility through senseless acts of inhumanity.

What is at the kernel of these contraries? How is it that such vast contraries sit side-by-side? If we are each authors of our lives, then what do we use as material to author such lives? This book seeks to make sense of these questions by theorizing a vast and interconnected system, in which each person is the key to the system. For various reasons that will become apparent, this system is conceived as a fractal system, a fractal being a pattern that repeats itself on different scales, and the power to alter it is theorized to reside with each person. It has been said: "Become the change you wish to see in the world" (quoted in, Potts 2002: A34). But how on earth can anything that one does have an impact on the whole earth, unless that is the implicit nature of the human–earth system. This book will explore the real power that each of us has, by examining the incredible fractal that connects the smallest entities in the system, with progressively larger constructs, finally culminating in the canvas of evolution itself.

If we are implicitly connected with the play of larger, more complex movements—whether of weather or markets or geopolitical stability—then it must be that who we are, what we say, and what we do, is ultimately creating the problems that seem so far removed, and conversely, who we are, what we say, and what we do, that can concretely and effectively solve these problems. It must also mean that the vast numbers of problems we find ourselves in, whether globally, nationally, regionally, or locally, are due to the continued misapplication or perhaps even lack of application of the power resident within us. Being a key part of the human–earth system, each of us influences it by our small acts and words daily, without realizing this. We do not realize the extent of the power we are invested with. Acting in the system, without knowledge of our actions on the system, creates the dichotomies that we are faced with today.

The first step, hence, is to gain clarity into the nature of the system. If we are a central part of a single human–earth system, then, by definition, realization of this will necessitate a significant shift in our conception of the system, since currently, we do not consider the system to be of such a nature. Such a re-conception may, as Einstein has suggested, allow us to solve life's problems, since as he observed, we cannot solve life's problems with the same consciousness that we have created them with. The consciousness that has created it is one of a lack of knowledge of what the system that we are an implicit part of is. The change in consciousness is the awakening to knowledge of what the system is, and consequently to a more guided play of what the result of our actions on the system is.

AN INTEGRATED FRACTAL SYSTEM

How is it that a shift in thought or attitude can have an impact on the whole world? It is fine to talk of a ripple effect or a viral effect. It is my sense, however, that the only way in which a shift at a small level—bounded by finite space and time—can have a profound effect on levels removed from it, is if the bounded space and time is intricately connected with everything around it, and further, is connected in such a manner that the nature of the shift is replicated in larger spaces progressively removed from it. A system of this nature, where a self-similar pattern repeats itself on different scales, is none other than a fractal. It is my contention, thus, that we are all connected by a ubiquitous fractal system, and it is by this nature of the system that profound shifts within ourselves can cause profound shifts in the world.

A variation of this idea has been amply explored by Mandelbrot (1982) and others at the material or physical level. Apparently, nature employs fractals in building many of her constructs. Thus, clouds, snowflakes, crystals, mountain ranges, lightning, river networks, blood vessels, coastlines, broccoli, amongst many other constructs have been created as fractals. There is an inherent simplicity and efficiency in this approach, since a small amount of information contained as a seed-pattern can be replicated on larger scale to build far more complex structures (Mandelbrot 1982). This idea is also highly consistent with Buckminster Fuller's work who explored the notion of nature as a highly efficient designer (Fuller 1982), employing techniques to minimize the use of energy. In this book, there is only a radical extension to the idea of employing fractal systems to physical systems, to apply it to complex behavioral systems such as persons, corporations, markets, and other complex systems. There has been some attempt by both Mandelbrot (Mandelbrot and Hudson 2004) and Elliott (Frost and Prechter 2001) to interpret financial markets in terms of fractals. It is worth noting here that both their approaches focus on change in numbers or physical patterns, and is a special or limited case of the fractal-model presented in this book. We will briefly review some of their key findings in light of the model presented later in the book.

By this very logic, it also becomes apparent why the systems we live in can remain so obstinately the same. For, unless there is a profound shift in the pattern that lies at the base of the fractal, the fractal will remain the same. In fact, the base pattern of the fractal, reinforced through a whole system or society that has grown from it, provides an easy mold within which to continue living out of the base pattern. It requires substantial effort to shift the base pattern, but once that is done, the effects inevitably impact the rest of the system.

We should also note that at the leading edge of science, fractals are being recognized as the patterns of chaos.[1] When we consider the vast contradictions abound in our world at first sight these come across as chaotic. On deeper examination though, as will become apparent through the course of this book, a deeper and, in fact, causative order will be observed in the fractals that peep through the veils of apparent chaos.

IN SEARCH OF THE BASE-PATTERN

If indeed we are part of a fractal system, then the critical observation is one of realizing what the pattern at the base of the fractal is. If this is not identified, then the fractal will never be known. If it is identified, then effective insight and power are potentially unlocked. One may look at a broccoli for hours, but unless one sees the self-similar broccolette repeating itself at progressively larger scales, the simplicity of the overall structure and the corresponding power to effectively alter it will remain a mystery. Further, if indeed we are part of a fractal system, then the "base-pattern" of the system must be apparent in plain sight; else it cannot be a fractal system. Hence, regardless of the scale we choose to focus on, the self-repeating pattern should be evident.

It follows that the pattern must exist in many facets of our history and our geography. While we could examine instances through history and across geography, we will leave such analyses for a later discussion in the book. For now and as the most fundamental of starting points possible, let us examine the deepest of our histories and amongst the vastest of our geographies—the relationship between the earth and the sun. By definition, such a starting-point would then be present as the play of history and geography unfolds. Imagine then the interaction between these defining entities through the ages. For eons the earth has revolved around the sun. In that revolution it has continually rotated around its own axis, thereby creating a rhythm of night and day, repeated again and again, endlessly. But looking more deeply at that rhythm, three distinct phases seem to characterize the day.

As the sun first breaks across the horizon, light is shed upon the constructs on the earth, and in that light there is an awareness of the boundary that defines each construct. Having woken up from slumber each form, as it were, becomes aware of what it is—there is an awakening to the *physical* structure that defines it. As the sun rises, the form becomes active, and in this process, it becomes clear as to what it is and what it stands for. The activity expresses its *vitality* and in this vitality there is interaction and experimentation, and the vast play of one life form with another. As the sun descends, so to speak, and countless stars emerge in the sky, it is as though the myopia that had bounded our focused actions through the day is removed, and we begin to see the stage of our day from many more perspectives. The phase of vitality yields to a phase of *mentality*, where a relative increase in introspection, reflection, and consideration of many more points of view comes into focus.

These three phases—physicality, vitality, mentality[2]—have repeated themselves day after day since the earth and the sun first began their mutual dance with each other. In this manner of seeing, just as the constant exposure to the sun has filled up life forms with solar energy, so too the play of the mutual earth–sun movement has embedded these three phases into the very fibers of life. Perhaps it is fair to say that the DNA of the earth, of circumstances on the earth, is imbued with the physical, vital, and mental phases.

PHYSICALITY, VITALITY, AND MENTALITY

But what really does it mean to exist in a physical phase, in practical terms? The emphasis in this phase is on the structure, on what is made visible by the first play of light on things, by what the eye first sees when it sees the object. It is not necessarily to see what the object is doing or expressing, but to see what the object is physically. The defining characteristic, the mantra of the phase can perhaps be thought of as "reality that is experienced by what one sees with the physical eye." The form is the focus, and it tends to be synonymous with the established order of things. It exists. It has a high measure of stability or even rigidity to it. Once established, it takes a substantial passage of time to alter it. In other words, change is marginal and can only occur in bounds or limits established by the structure. The structure has to be the basis of the change, and even when change does occur, it is incremental.

Thus, in the larger play of life the basis is seen as the physical form. It is the interaction of form with form that creates other possibilities. This is the basis of creativity. Bring two gases together, for instance, and they will react in a particular way because it is the nature of the form of one gas to react in that precise manner with the form of another. Bring two children together, and it is the nature of the form that will cause them to play with each other. Bring two animals together, and depending on what type they are, they will play with, threaten, or devour the other. The system is a function of physical form, and just as there are fixed forms, so too, there are fixed laws that accompany the individual behavior of each form, and the interaction when one form is brought into proximity with another. In this view, nothing can change, because what is, is already determined by the form, the laws that accompany that form and the law that accompanies the interaction of form. In this play of life, if there is creativity, it is confined to the boundaries of the myriad laws already in place. Hence, it is marginal.

In the vital phase, the emphasis is on assertion of energy. In this phase, the life-constructions are absorbed in dynamic activity. They then exercise their faculties in the play of life. Life-constructions seek to assert themselves and grow through experimentation. It is as though the energy of the sun is translated into an abundance of different kinds of energies. Each form, relatively dormant at the break of day, finds its innate energies being released and exercised. This phase is about the interaction of energies. Some energies overpower others. Some express themselves in harmony with others. Some combine with others to create new forms of energies. The searching and humming of bees interacts with the attractiveness of flowers. People and markets seek to grow in whatever ways they can. All is alive with activity, and in this activity the character and characteristics of each gets expressed and in one way or the other, is refined. The mantra of this phase is more likely "reality as experienced by assertiveness and the myriad play of energies."

In the larger play of life, thus, it is assertiveness and energy that dominate. The energy of each seeks to assert itself at any cost. It seeks to gather more energy by any means and to establish its rule over other forms that it may have a base by which to continue to increase its energy and exercise its assertiveness. There is vast experimentation in this phase, but it is not driven by thought or by order. There is a devouring to devour, a conquering to conquer, and it is perhaps the strongest and longest-lasting energy that triumphs in the end. There is constant change of form in this configuration, but the essential drive remains at self-assertion and conquest. Change will continue to occur as long as some forms' assertiveness is accomplished in the bargain.

The phase of mentality is characterized by an increase of introspection, reflection, and assimilation. It is as though with the dawning of the stars, the focus has shifted from the here and now, to the mysteries of the unknown. What does one stand for? What will happen tomorrow? Who is one in the play of life? Why did today unroll the way it did? Such questioning leads to the meaning and perhaps even the trajectory of one's activities becoming clearer, and, that which one is secretly or even overtly working towards comes more to the surface. Such questioning leads to a progressive understanding of the meaning of not only one's self, but of others in the vast play of life. And that questioning, to a deeper recognition that all forms exist for a reason, just as self exists for a purpose, leads to an understanding of all other selves. In such thought, the purpose of form and energy can also become clearer. The mantra of this phase is perhaps best characterized as "life as experienced by thought and the idea."

PERMUTATIONS OF THE PATTERN'S BUILDING-BLOCKS

The three fundamental building-blocks of the all-present pattern are hypothesized to be this physicality, vitality, and mentality. These building-blocks can occur separately or in different configurations, and depending on the explicit permutation, forms one of several seed-states that becomes the active kernel within us. That kernel then, through its implicit fractal power gives birth to the reality that settles around each living being. When we talk of the contradictions of life around us, we will see, as the book develops, that it is the play of different fractal realities emanating from different seed-states that creates this condition. It is also, perhaps, the contradiction between the one implicit ubiquitous fractal, that we have yet to discover, and the myriad fractals so created from many different seed-states that also creates the vast contraries juxtaposed amongst each other.

A kernel formed from the pure physical state would see the world as fixed and the notion of change beyond marginal limits as impossible. A kernel formed from a pure vital state would see the world as a constant flux of random energies dominated by a particular energy determined by the strength of energy. A kernel formed from a pure mental state would see the world as a changing and progressive play of ideas and ideals. But there could also be a combination of states that forms the kernels. Hence, it could be that a state dominates, and others, in a manner of speaking, serve it. It could be that the vital and mental states serve the physical state. In this permutation, the energies of the vital, and the thought-power of the mental, would be subservient to the status quo embodied by the physical state. In such a situation, all would be a play of prolonging yesterday's laws and glories, through enforcement of energy and power, and through rationalization of thought. Or, it could be that the physical and mental powers are subservient to the vital state. Then, it would be the strongest energy that would lead in the play of life always, with physical structures being created to support this, and the power of mind being used to rationalize why a dominant energy needs to lead and being used to advance the play of that energy. Or it could be that the mental stance leads, with the physical and vital powers supporting its play. In this case, it would be idea that leads, and physical structure and vital energy that offer themselves in advancement of the leading idea or the ideal.

Each of these combinations could live as kernels within individuals and collectivities; by fractal pressure these can create the practical reality that those individuals and collectivities are embedded in. In such a case, when these different practical realities meet or intersect, vast contraries could come into existence. So long as individuals and collectivities are separate, the corresponding practical realities work themselves according to the seed-state resident in them. Until quite recently, for example, much of our world functioned in isolated blocks, which also perhaps gave these seed-states a chance to express the possibilities resident within them more completely. Hence, we may find that some countries such as the USA developed along more physical or material lines, as compared with other countries such as India that, relatively speaking, have developed along more mental lines. However, through rapid advancement of technology, increasing globalization, and increasing cosmopolitanism, the world has become more of a melting pot and thus, different practical realities are pressed against one another to create a number of vast contraries. But it may even be that some overarching fractal reality is using seeming contraries to work out its own reality more effectively. This process will be examined in more detail later.

THE BASE PHYSICAL–VITAL–MENTAL PATTERN

One can see that the fundamental building blocks either in isolation or in specific combination with one another can be the basis of a seed-state; it then creates a reality consistent with its seed. At the first sight, one could make the case for any of these combinations being the fundamental base-pattern we had started our exploration of the fractal with, that is, physical, vital, mental combining in any order whatsoever. If, however, we revisit the earth–sun dance in which the physical, vital, and mental states had arisen, and if we use the movement of the sun as the key to discover the potential order of the three fundamental states, we will see that the fractal-pattern must be the progressive movement through the physical, vital, and mental states, in order. As the sun interacts with the earth, it does so in a manner where the physical state yields to the vital state which then yields to the mental state. Hence, it is a progression through these three states in the mentioned order that becomes the base fractal pattern. One must remember, this is important because this is what is embedded in the DNA of life.

In another way of seeing, it is as though each of the phases feeds into the other and is a fundamental part of the whole that defines how each form comes into its own. It does not make sense to speak of one phase without referring to the others. Consider the example of a seed becoming a flower. One may think of the seed as being the physical beginning. It appears dormant and has precise boundaries observable with the eye. The phase of vitality is characterized by movement. Tendrils reach out. The play of energies accelerates. The tendrils move towards the sun, the roots from the seed move deeper into the earth. There is more give and take—gases, water, and nutrients enter into the seed— tendril structure, and other compounds are simultaneously released. At the culmination of this, a flower emerges, and it is at this stage that the meaning of the seed becomes clear. This is its identity, what it has stood for secretly in the play of things. This is its expression in the play of things. Yet, it required a passage through the three phases—physical, vital, mental—to express that identity.

But imagine if the movement did not culminate in the reality of the flower, that is, the journey through the three states had been forestalled. Then the possibility inherent in that creation would not be fully realized. Certainly, something would have been created, for that appears to be the implicit characteristic of life, but it would have been only a shadow of what was possible. Now imagine that the many movements across the earth are not necessarily unfolding along the physical–vital–mental path, and further, that there are many movements that are in fact headed in the opposite or in lateral directions. What kind of earth would this create? Likely, one filled with many, many contradictions.

In the earth–sun dance, it is the interaction of the sun with the earth that creates a fundamental triplicity that forms have to journey through. This triplicity starts from the physical state, and if we objectively view the relative timing when humans, the potential mental-beings, appeared on the earth-scene, we find it is recent. Hence, it is as though the existing triplicity itself is biased toward the physical state. That is, the vitality and mentality seem more in service of the physicality than the other way round. The fractal so created has taken on more of a characteristic of obstinately-fortified structures prolonging the law of yesteryear. Hence, as strong as the natural physical–vital–mental path defined by the movement of the sun in the earth–sun system is, it appears to be constantly held back by a long-standing fractal pointed in the other direction that seeks to maintain the rule of yesteryear. It is as though this opposition of fractals has created a rite of passage that we humans, potential mental-beings, must pass through, in order to arrive at a realization of our identity. It is as though in order to cross through this rite of passage the power of mentality and, hence, individuality must begin to shine in us, and the physical and vital powers must gladly offer themselves in service of the growing mentality, or emergence of our individuality. When this happens, then the new-born power causes old orders to crumble, and the meaning of individuality and its inevitable impact on bringing about progressive change in the world becomes apparent. One must note that we are not saying that this mentality is the secret of our identity; we are saying that with the expression of mentality that identity becomes clearer.

In the dance of the earth with the sun, the physical–vital–mental triplicity is reinforced daily. Yet, at the end of each day, there is a period of night that precedes the journeying of the next day. Perhaps it is a deeper rest and assimilation that occurs during that time, so that when the new dawn emerges, each construct approaches the journey from a slightly new vantage point. Thus, not only is there a movement through three phases in a particular order, there is a general intention of progress that seems to accompany it. In the vaster scheme of things, it is almost as though the earth itself uses the passage defined by the triplicity to arrive at a reality in which the triplicity is itself transformed by the increasing light of the sun, thereby becoming another earth entirely. What is the notion of identity in this? Is it that some implicit identity uses circumstance to define itself? This notion will be explored further.

SUMMARY

We have so far focused on identifying the fundamental pattern of a potentially ubiquitous fractal. We identified fundamental building-blocks of the pattern, and further suggested that there is a meaningful order to the building-blocks which when arranged becomes the fundamental pattern that should be evident in any field of life. Such observations will be made in further chapters of this book. We have also suggested that it is possible to create fractals through a different combination of the fundamental building-blocks, and that when fractals emanating from these building-blocks play themselves out, it results in vast contradictions in the play of life. In fact, the mental stage, being relatively recent, implies that even the ubiquitous fractal has a bias towards physicality in its natural expression. This creates an inherent opposition to progress. We have suggested that the opposition of these contrary fractals to the one ubiquitous and sun-marked fractal forms a rite of passage, and in actively engaging this passage, true and progressive individualities are born. It is with the birth of such individualities that real and progressive change happens, and that the power resident in one's self can be seen to have a real effect on positive changes in the world. Though figuratively, we have suggested that the "earth" and the "sun" are real actors in the unfolding of life, and perhaps, somehow, give context and meaning to a ubiquitous fractal that may emerge or stand behind things, the role of "earth" and "sun" and individuality, and the purpose of the ubiquitous fractal are yet to be explored. This too will be discussed in subsequent chapters.

While these suggestions are hypotheses at this point, as we progress, these will be marked out by further observations. Nonetheless, we will use this pattern and possibility as our starting point.

2

The Person Pattern

CONCEPT RECAP AND INTRODUCTION

In Chapter 1, we hypothesized that there is a ubiquitous fractal that connects the individual with the entire earth system. It is by virtue of this fractal that the individual has the power to bring about meaningful change in the world. While the notion of "meaningful" will be further developed through the course of the book, we already know from the discussion made in the last chapter that at the least this could mean the overcoming of contrary fractals emanating from potentially discordant kernels or base-patterns in one's self. It could also mean the awakening or mobilization of the sun-marked physical–vital–mental base pattern within one's self, by virtue of which the deeply embedded yesteryear-oriented earth-fractal can progressively be overcome. This is no trivial task and marks a rite of passage that will likely awaken something significant in the being.

This chapter begins with an examination of what the potential fractal building-blocks—physical, vital, mental—mean at the level of the person. We will then examine how these building-blocks might combine with one another to create different "personalities" or "tendencies" or "habits" that define who one is, consequently also blocking other possibilities in the being. In the context of these tendencies we will examine what the sun-marked physical–vital–mental movement might signify, and what might get released if this were to become a person's modus operandi. We will also look at what kind of pattern tends to emerge as one moves through one's life.

THE ARCHITECTURE OF A PERSON

In the earth–sun dance, the structure of a day is marked by three phases. Applying a similar architecture to each of the three fundamental building-blocks, thereby also beginning to test if the easily evident fractal can indeed be used to arrive at a more complete conception of things, would mean that there are perhaps three ways to interpret the terms, physical, vital, mental, in the context of a person. In the previous chapter, we had suggested that "physical" referred to structures that the eye can see, "vital" referred to energy flows of various kinds, and "mental" referred to thought and ideas. Let us, hence, use each of these orientations to hopefully gain more insight into each of three terms as they apply to a person, that is, starting with the "physical" or structure-based orientation, let us focus on the terms physical, vital, mental. Then let us use the "vital" and "mental" orientations to revisit each of the three terms.

Under the physical orientation, "physical" would refer to the body itself. "Vital" would refer to the energy or flows in the body, whether of blood, nerve impulses, passage and digestion of foods, and flow of air, amongst other vital flows. "Mental" would refer to the intelligence embedded in the body by which each sub-system integrates holistically with the body system.

In the vital or energy-based orientation, we are broadly focusing on self-referencing flows of energy. Hence, at the "physical" level, such states of being would be ones that focused attention on the body, such as fatigue or inertia on the negative side, and flexibility or strength or dexterity on the positive side. At the "vital" level, states of being would be the ones which, though primarily self-referencing, tended to be sparked by or to engender interaction with others. On the negative side, such states of being might be anger, depression, doubt, fear, jealousy, pride, amongst others. On the positive side, such states of being might be courage, determination, humility, joy, gratitude, amongst others. At the "mental" level states of being would be related to the thought. Hence, on the negative side, these may be anxiety, mental noise, perturbing thoughts, and short-sightedness, amongst others. On the positive side, states of being might be more systematic thinking, increase of imagination, ability to synthesize with the caveat that this would take place with a bias around self-positioning or self-referencing, rather than for the sake of pure knowledge itself.

Mental or thought-based orientation would refer to basic perceptions about oneself and the world. Hence, the "physical" level would refer to the notion that life and its possibilities are a function of physical structures. Life and thought emerge from physical reality and all possibilities are a function of form. Change must be dictated by what is possible at the level of form. The "vital" level would refer to the notion that life and its possibilities are a function of energies and interaction of energies. Assertiveness of energy, conquest of one energy by another, possible combination of energies would be the rules of the game, and change would be driven by whatever energy was on the rise at the moment. The "mental" level would refer to the notion that life and its possibilities are a function of thoughts, ideas, and ideals. Possibility would be dictated by what thought can conceive. Physical form and play of energy cannot restrain thought. Thought is the master and change can occur at the speed of thought.

Hence, having applied the three building-blocks of the ubiquitous fractal to each of the building blocks, results in a more robust and elaborate definition of each of the elements in the context of a person. If when randomly asked a person were to define herself, she might suggest that she was an accumulation or conglomeration of the body, feelings and emotions, and thoughts. Applying the building-blocks to each of these, however, results in a more complete sense of what each of these is, as we have just seen. This should not be surprising, given that we are hypothesizing that the three elements are embedded in the fiber of life, and hence application of them in elaborating or thinking about any construct must result in a more complete definition of what the construct stands for. The physical, vital, and mental building-blocks, hence, have provided a basis of definition or at least partial definition of a person. This definition is summarized in Figure 2.1.

FIGURE 2.1 Architecture of a Person

	Orientation		
	Physical	Vital	Mental
Physical	Body	Physical states of being	Structure-based outlook
Vital	Bodily-flows	Emotional states of being	Energy-based outlook
Mental	Body-intelligence	Mental states of being	Thought-based outlook

Building-blocks

Source: Author

In very relevant research conducted over the period of 20 years, Sandra Seagal, a school teacher and psychotherapist, identified three distinct sounds in each person's voice. These sounds were of a high, middle, and low frequency, respectively.

Segal's research (Seagal and Horne 1997) identified that the high frequency expressed the mental function, the middle frequency the emotional or vital function, and the low frequency the physical function. Further, patterns in the voice comprised of these three sounds, paralleled distinct patterns in people's behavior and process. That is, people with a particular physical, vital, and mental make-up as identified by the voice, displayed parallel physical, vital, and mental dynamics in their behavior and process. This is a pertinent illustration of a physical, vital, mental building-block based fractal.

CREATION OF TENDENCIES

A more elaborate range of possibility resident in each of these blocks or states has been fleshed out through application of the physical, vital, and mental lenses. Yet, there will be peculiar and particular projections based on what is active or what leads in these states. In other words, the particular kernels or base-patterns in the person, through force of fractal pressure, will create a reality consistent with that kernel(s). We know that the kernels will be comprised of one of or some combination of each of the three fundamental building-blocks. Depending on what part leads, the kernel will either be in alignment with the ubiquitous fractal or will be in opposition to it. In a person, however, the situation is made more complex because of the many combinatorial variations in the vital and mental beings. Hence, there are two levels that need to be looked at. Let us consider a few examples to illustrate this potential complexity.

Imagine someone who has a great love for food. At some point during the person's development, there may have been an association of satisfaction through eating. In terms of the interaction of the basic building-blocks, it is entirely possible that there is a physical element in the being that feels its reality from continuing to imbibe various foods. There is then a vital element attached to it, say a feeling of happiness or joy associated with eating. There may be a mental element attached to it where the person is planning what their next meal could be or even what they need to do in order to earn money to buy food. It seems like these basic building-blocks then join together, either through habit or perhaps some other process, to create a tendency of some sort. This tendency becomes a kernel in the person and through virtue of the creativity embedded in each of the building-blocks, and, therefore, in the tendency itself, it imposes its own reality that emanates out like a fractal. That tendency exists to fulfill its reality. The person who houses this tendency, thus, will most likely spend a fair amount of his time planning for food, because he knows that eating gives him pleasure.

Or, consider, that as a child grows he sees displays of anger in his house. He also sees how those who exercise anger seem to get their way in the end. In this instance, anger, a vital element becomes the lead. There is a mental element attached to it—the thought that if one needs to accomplish something one needs to exercise anger in order to change circumstances. This vital–mental combination settles into habit and in doing so, attracts some kind of physical structure or sheath around it to give it permanence. This anger-based vital–mental–physical tendency now also exists, and like other creations, seeks to fulfill the meaning of its reality through exercising its raison d'être at every possible opportunity.

Let us consider another example of someone who loves to read philosophy. Perhaps it was the love for ideas that dawned on this person. This was the mental element. The joy that this activity provided drew energy to support the act of reading. This joy-energy vital-conglomerate then became the vital element supporting the mental element. Force of habit drew some kind of physical structure to it, to give it permanence. This mental–vital–physical tendency, hence, came into existence, and like any other tendency seeks to continue to perpetuate itself.

There are hundreds of opportunities for tendencies of this nature to come into existence within a person. The passage of life is a continual exchange between a person and his environment, and in that exchange, it will perhaps be the norm that the substance and norms of life will incarnate in the substance of the person. In another way of putting this, there are many fractals that exist in the world, and as one enters into proximity with them, it is highly likely that materials, tendencies, or kernels, pass from those fractals into the person. This is perhaps how the nature of the world is perpetuated. It cannot be any other way if there is reality to the fractal nature. For a kernel in some being somewhere exists to propagate itself—that is its nature. It is also the nature of constructs of Nature to receive these influences, and often to imbibe them.

THE ALTERATION OF TENDENCIES

It is only when the sun-marked physical–vital–mental fractal becomes active in one that there is a counter-force that can alter the balance of the world's natural exchange with its creatures. It requires something of a different nature than the existing nature to alter it. It is hypothesized, through eons of habit, that the existing nature is a fractal led by the physical component more than anything else, and is, therefore, effectively pointed in the opposite direction to the ubiquitous sun-marked physical–vital–mental fractal. Hence, it is only when the sun-marked fractal can become active in one's self that there is the possibility of the normal flow of exchange to change. The normal flow is one of circumstance, or environment, or norms in society, or exercise of other personalities imparting something of their substance into the person. It is only when the person becomes an individual, a truly creative entity in the scheme of things, that this flow is reversed. It is then that something unique from within the person can begin to flow from within and alter external circumstances.

While considering oneself, one is, practically speaking, a being constituent of several habits. And these habits, as we have just seen, are emanations or the nature of tendencies that exist within oneself. One wakes up in the morning, and depending on the nature of sleep one had, and the perceived demands of the day, there may be some of several tendencies that exercise themselves: one calling to attention the disturbed sleep one just had—a tendency whose core is vital, frustration, and whose mental-element is the play of theories as to why this was, and what could be done to promote a better sleep. Another tendency surfacing the fear with a presentation to be given later in the day. A third tendency exhibiting haste because one is already 10 minutes late, and so on. Later in the day one walks into a room, and even if one felt quite grounded prior to that, the active vibrations of the other fractals swirling in that space and emanating from other people there, pull one into one or more different orbits, or surfaces matching tendencies from the host of "guests" one houses within oneself.

Who is one, in all this? In the mutual earth–sun dance, the progression of the sun through the day marks a movement through three phases—the physical, the vital, and the mental. This in itself is not the identity, but the identity is revealed through this progression. The myriad tendencies in our selves clamber for their own expression, often at any cost. "So long as my desire is fulfilled right now," says one tendency, "I do not care for any consequences to myself or to another." This is repeated by so many of these small voices, so many times a day, that even if one had a unique identity, it seems to recede into or to be left in the background. But what if the same pattern of progression as embodied by the sun-marked physical–vital–mental pattern is similarly applied to each of the tendencies? Would this allow identity to reveal itself? Let us look at this more closely.

Let us pick up one of the tendencies already considered, say the one of anger. This tendency is led by the vital element of anger. This is the nexus of its being and it is organized around this. Even though it has a mental element, one that believed that the exercise of anger is necessary to achieve things, it is not the same thing as altering the nature of the nexus in accordance with the progression exhibited by the sun-marked physical–vital–mental fractal. Hence, each time that this tendency exercised itself, if one could in a manner of speaking detach oneself from the active experience or the lure of its reality, one might be able to impose upon it another way of being. Perhaps progressive thought can be imposed upon the tendency to persuade it that more complete reason must be used each time that anger arises. Hence, through rationality, the accompanying mental element can perhaps be persuaded that anger in itself is not the way that one's plans can be fulfilled. That tendency can be given a stronger and truly more rational mental element, by which the raison d'être of the tendency is altered.

The main point is that the fractal that this tendency is exhibiting is pointed in a direction contrary to what we are hypothesizing to be the ubiquitous fractal. So organized, it perpetuates its own reality, and by definition cannot progress. In fact, it will likely strengthen its tendency to assert itself, always allocating or drawing more mental, vital, physical elements to strengthen its central nexus of anger. By contrast, if a willingness to alter its components by yielding control to more progressive mental elements is admitted, its fundamental milieu is altered, and progress becomes possible.

When such tendencies admit of the paradigm of progress, a totally different dynamic is set up in a person. We are not implying that progress is synonymous with being in a mental state all the time. In fact, as we have hinted at, and will hopefully make more concrete as the materials in this book develop, that the physical, the vital, and the mental are all crucial components of a full existence, and each in fact needs the other not only for its own completeness, but also for the completeness of the whole. It is the nature of the organization that is of importance. And what we are suggesting as a paradigm of progressive and currently needed organization is embodied by what we are terming as the sun-marked physical–vital–mental fractal.

This marks a progression of one stage to another in the order of physical to vital to mental, because as each of these powers of organization currently stands, a mental orientation allows the notion of progressive questioning and an idea-driven life, and at its limits, perhaps even movements such as intuition, inspiration, and revelation, that hint at or show always more clearly the limits of current constructs and the possibilities that may exist if one were to truly continue a paradigm of progress.

Thus, when we have myriad tendencies within oneself, which in reality are expressions of a stagnated way of being, how is it possible to enter into a phase of true questioning? The questions can be so many and their power is in opening up the being to possibilities. But if we do not even reach that level of human possibility where established structures, established contraries, and established tendencies are questioned, how can we possibly move beyond them? If there is something else that life can offer us, how would we know that unless we are willing to ask the question? If the way that we are living is incomplete, if there are hidden powers and potentialities that are waiting to manifest, how would we know that, unless we are willing to ask the question. But the question itself is not what is important, it is the attitude and the meaning of asking the question that is important. Do we ask because we truly do not know? Or do we ask because of some intellectual curiosity. In our progress, we must reach the stage of realizing that there are mysteries, perhaps pointed to by such a thing as a ubiquitous sun-marked physical–vital–mental fractal that opens us from the inside to a new level of possibilities.

In its essence, the "physical" seems to indicate that which has already been manifested. The mantra of the physical, reminds us, of being "that which the eye can see." This marks the stability or the foundation on which future edifices may be constructed. This is the established order of things and is the result of all the efforts of the past. The "vital," on the other hand, seems to indicate the present. There are a play of energies and forces tussling with one another to establish their respective rules of law. One must recall that the mantra of the vital is "reality as experienced by the myriad play of energies." But what do these energies represent? In many instances, it could possibly be yesterday's structures seeking to prolong their rule into tomorrow. In many instances, it is tomorrow's possibilities seeking to establish their forms today. That energy which wins today will establish itself tomorrow. The "mental" by contrast, indicates the future. The mantra of this level is "life as driven by ideas." And this hints at myriad possibilities. Seek refuge in the mind and this is where one can find release from the constriction of today. This is where one can soar on flights of fancy and imagine what is possible tomorrow. This is the great force that can analyze and be critical and open passageways into dreams and visions that ultimately become the essence of life. Tomorrow's realities are today's ideas.

Hence, we are saying that at the level of person, a general paradigm of the physical orientation yielding to the vital orientation yielding to the mental orientation is what is required to avoid stagnation. Avoiding stagnation implies that the myriad voices and habits emanating from yesteryear-pointed tendencies lose their hold over one's reality, thereby allowing other deeper possibilities to surface. If there is something one stands for, if there is uniqueness in one's self, it can never come to the surface unless all the easily-surfacing movements lose their hold. These are those movements that live in established reality, either in one's self or in larger environments, and often represent a backward-pointing orientation rather than a progressive one. In allowing these to progress, thereby changing or dissolving them, something other than the common reality of yesterday has a chance of manifesting itself.

Depending on how far one is able to penetrate within oneself, it seems plausible that radically-different possibilities could emerge. If one, for instance, were able to change or dissolve a small number of tendencies, then potentially a small number of new tendencies would manifest. Perhaps these new tendencies are born from new thoughts and attitudes that one would prefer to exercise. If, on the other hand, one were able to do a deeper level of work and change or dissolve a much larger number of tendencies, then one might find that one's effective personality, of who one is, has drastically changed. In such a case, something that one is deep within oneself, inherently, may manifest. Not ideas and attitudes adopted from some bestseller or popular new-age movement, but something that one inherently is within oneself, with powerful innate feelings, thoughts, and a unique way of being. This then could become the active kernel or base-pattern of one's life, and emanate out as a truly creative fractal, one that potentially altered life in the world. That is the point of this book.

THE EMERGENCE OF IDENTITY

As one considers the vast number of tendencies that exist within each person, a general question that arises is why the manifestation of these tendencies varies by person, especially if, as we are hypothesizing, birth of tendencies is generally a function of commerce with life. While there may be general tendencies that exist in all people, one person exhibits an almost unique combination of tendencies when compared with any other. Why is this so? This could be so that there is a certain uniqueness embedded in each person that works itself out through the play of tendencies resident in that person. By overcoming, or causing progress of, or opening out these tendencies to the possibility of a general physical–vital–mental progression, it could be that what one stands for in one's self, gradually has a chance to manifest itself. Each person's rite of passage, though constituted of a general opposition comprised of a number of self-born and backward-pointing fractals to the general physical–vital–mental fractal, is yet unique in the precise constituents of the opposing fractals. Overcoming the unique combination of contraries requires manifestation of a unique combination of inherent strengths or powers, which once manifested forms the basis of a new being, in general alignment with the ubiquitous sun-marked physical–vital–mental fractal.

It follows that the sign of not living from one's uniqueness or core identity would mean that a person is continually afflicted by yesteryear-pointed tendencies that generate a mediocre living involved with trifle emotions, small wants and deeds, and habitual thoughts that one cannot really call one's own. Living one's uniqueness, on the other hand, would be marked by the absence of such trivialities, and would potentially be accompanied by such dynamics as are the stuff of identity. This is provided as a separate and deeper examination later in the book. It is also worthwhile reflecting on what ideal identities or kernels would be, if say, one were at the helm of a corporation, or a country, or even if were an artist, a musician, a writer, or an engineer, amongst other professions.

In the previous chapter, we had indicated that the physical–vital–mental pattern, if it is truly the base-pattern of a ubiquitous fractal, must be evident in all aspects of life almost automatically. If we were to observe the general tendency of a person's life, we would see that such a pattern emerges by itself. Hence, in one's younger days, one is more concerned with establishing a secure base for life—ensuring that one has money, food, and security for one's self and one's family. This is the physical phase. Later, perhaps in middle age, the general tendency is to experiment more. Once one has secured the basis of life, one is freer to assert one's self, and engage other energies, knowing that there is a basis of security on which to act. Hence, there is a wider interaction with people, and more of a coming into one's own rhythm of life. This is the vital phase. Finally, after one has played in life, there is more of an introspective phase that dawns—a questioning of what really it is all about, and an opening to deeper mysteries and possible realities, and perhaps even a reinterpretation of self in context to the larger picture. This is the mental phase.

Not surprisingly, this passage through life is consistent with Maslow's psychology (Maslow 1943) of the human being, embodied in his Hierarchy of Needs that puts needs in a ladder-like or more precisely a pyramid-structure, with physiological and safety needs—the "physical"—at the bottom, belonging and esteem—the "vital" phase—in the middle, and what he referred to as self-actualization—the "mental" phase—at the top. It was not that all human beings stepped through all phases of the pyramid. Rather, once one had taken care of the "lower" needs, then one was free to climb to higher needs. In fact, the lower needs, once fulfilled, provided the foundation by which the higher needs could exercise themselves. Whether he realized it or not, his model is a manifestation of the base-pattern in our hypothesized ubiquitous sun-marked physical–vital–mental fractal, and also an expression of how truer identity emerges.

In our earth–sun metaphor, it is as though earth stood for a progressive being that grows through overcoming various obstacles that have their basis in the physical, vital, and mental building-blocks. It is as though in going through passages defined by the interaction of various physical, vital, and mental elements, that the combination and general orientation of these building-blocks can alter, giving rise to an enhanced physical, vital, mental combination. In a certain sense, it is as though the earth were expressing itself through continually and progressively changing physical, vital, and mental masks. The changing masks themselves seem to be changing to imbibe more of the nature of the sun. What started off as self-centered, small, myopic, seems, through the action of the earth–sun dance, to be assuming more of the nature of the sun, that is, to become more timeless, vast, self-radiating. But this should not be surprising. In this metaphor, or model, the sun has assumed a central place. Physicality, vitality, mentality assume meaning as a result of it, and perhaps are manifestations, on earth, of basic principles of its being. Perhaps through the mutual earth–sun dance, the earth becomes an earth–sun. Perhaps that is the meaning of identity and of uniqueness, and perhaps all obstacles are shadow-states which when opened out to the natural progression marked by the sun's movement across a day on earth, reveal that identity, that is, the unique play of the sun in each formation of the earth.

The manifestation of uniqueness or identity by definition becomes a creative force in the world. This is the notion of creation. By fractal pressure anything that is created has its impact on the world. When the tendencies, which we had referred to earlier, are created, they are just reinforcing what already existed, and, therefore, their impact may not necessarily be felt because what they reinforce is what we are already used to. When something new is created, however, its effects are felt immediately. It becomes a force for change in the world. Hence, the true act of creativity is to be able to create something new in oneself. And life offers us hundreds of opportunities in a day to work towards this. Each time the action of a yesteryear-pointing tendency is felt, if we were able to recognize this, and allow a movement of progress to infuse it, something of the innate uniqueness resident in each of us may be able to reveal a little more of itself.

SUMMARY

In this chapter, we began by considering what physical, vital, and mental may mean in the context of a person. We found that application of the physical, vital, and mental building-blocks to each of these orientations in fact resulted in a more elaborate definition of a person. We found that self-organizing combinations of these basic building-blocks resulted in myriad tendencies that through fractal pressure created the reality that a person may experience. We hypothesized that each of these self-organized fractals, drawn from the existing order of things, acts in general opposition to the sun-marked physical–vital–mental fractal, and "addressing" these self-organizing fractals or tendencies becomes a rite of passage by which truer identity can manifest. We hypothesized that "addressing" each of these tendencies is synonymous to opening them out to the sun-marked physical–vital–mental pattern that allows the tendency to partake of progress. Such progress, we hypothesized, is like imbibing more of the characteristic of the sun into each formation on earth. By virtue of its creation and the fractal reality that accompanies it, this truer identity becomes a force for change in the world.

How this change works in the world will be discussed in the chapters to follow.

3

The Business Pattern

INTRODUCTION

As in the previous chapter, we will begin our explorations of the ubiquitous fractal in the business world with clarification on the meaning of the terms physical, vital, and mental in the business world. We will look at how the different building-blocks can combine in different ways to create a very differently run business. We will also examine the necessity of the integration of all the building-blocks in thinking about the running of a corporation. Finally, we will examine the link between the fractal at the personal level and the business level, thereby beginning to make a logical case for the existence of the hypothesized fractal model.

ARCHITECTURE OF BUSINESS

When we began to interpret the meaning of physical, vital, and mental at the level of person, we applied the components of the sun-marked physical–vital–mental fractal pattern to each building-block independently to arrive at a more robust sense for what each building-block could mean at the level of the person. Remembering the physical mantra—"what the eye can see"—let us extrapolate what such an application could mean for the "physical" aspect or component of a business.

Under the physical umbrella, the "physical" state would refer to tangible, material assets possessed by a corporation. To elaborate, this may mean equipment, buildings, land, inventories, and product. The "vital" state, under a physical umbrella or orientation, would refer to assets that represented tangible, touchable energy, such as money or available cash of a company. The "mental" state would represent assets of an intangible nature such as the brand, the goodwill, and the intellectual property of the company. We had suggested earlier that the physical represents the past, the result of all the ideas and energies that had played out to create the foundation of tomorrow's world. Assets are such a representation of the past results of organizational action, and therefore belong to the physical realm.

Recalling the vital mantra—"the play of energies"—let us extrapolate what that could mean for a business. Under a vital umbrella or orientation, the "physical" state would refer to the flow of goods, transportation networks, telecommunications networks, and other tangible networks that a corporation may possess. The "vital" state would refer to the flow of energies, comprising such energies as financial assets—cash flows, costs, sales, profits, return on investments—and the flow of emotion at the employee, customer, and other stakeholder levels. Flow of emotion captures an important part of the intangible experience that any party interacting within or with the company may experience. As at the level of the person, all these flows are primarily self-referencing, that is, they exist to aggrandize the conception of self or in this case of corporation. In the case of financial flows, the emphasis is on what the corporation must do in order to ensure these continue to aggrandize the corporation. In the case of experience, similarly, what must be done so that the employee or customer affirms or reinforces the dynamics of the corporation. The "mental" state would refer to flows at the level of thought or of concept. Hence, what are the processes or the flows by which intellectual property, or brand value, or goodwill is created? Who is involved, and how does this type of value get created by the interactions between those involved.

Remembering the mental mantra—"reality as shaped by thought"—let us explore its implications for the business. Under such an umbrella or orientation, the "physical" would refer to the notion of a fixed world. Key ideas about what is possible in the marketplace would be dictated by the notion that "what the eye can see" is what is possible. Hence, corporate strategy or corporate possibility would be a function of the fixed nature of things. Whatever had made the corporation successful in the past is what will make it successful in the future. If a corporation has failed in the past, it simply would need to emulate another that had been successful in the fixed world, to become successful. "Vital," on the other hand, would refer to the notion of a variable world, in which assertion of energy is going to determine successful outcome. Nothing is fixed in this orientation: success is a function of asserting the corporation through financial means. The boundaries of the world, in this kind of orientation, are much more fluid. Processes, strategies, products, do not need to remain essentially the same, as in the physical orientation. Anything can change so long as financial success and stakeholder's success, defined in terms of financial impact, is upheld. It will be possible to go into new markets, new geographies, new products, with new people and new processes if need be, in order to ensure that the all-important financial return is assured. "Mental" would refer to a world driven by thought and idea. The primary impetus for driving a corporation would not even be financial returns, under this outlook, but idea and ideal. Needless to say, this kind of world would potentially be the most variable. Not even the constraint on ensuring financial returns would necessarily impede it. Hence, such a corporation would potentially much more easily change product, process, market, geography, if the idea that drove it demanded that kind of action in return.

The "architecture" of a business is summarized in Figure 3.1.

FIGURE 3.1   Architecture of a Business

| | | Orientation | | |
		Physical	Vital	Mental
Building-blocks	Physical	Tangible asset such as land	Tangible networks such as transportation	Fixed world, processes, approach
	Vital	Tangible energy such as cash	Flows of energy such as financial assets and customer experience	Variable world; assertion through financial means
	Mental	Intangible asset such as goodwill	Flow facilitating creation of intangible assets	Idea-driven and higher fluidity

Source: Author

Hence, while more fully defining the architecture of a day in the initial earth–sun analogy and also defining the "architecture" of a person, the physical, vital, and mental building-blocks can quite completely define the architecture of a business. There must, as such, be some validity to applying them to an organization in the business world.

PERMUTATIONS OF THE PHYSICAL, VITAL, MENTAL BUILDING-BLOCKS

As in the case of a person, different combinations of building-blocks will yield different kernels which through fractal pressure will tend to create different guiding and operating realities for businesses.

Stringing corresponding components of each orientation together, for example, yields a "purer" physical, vital, mental state, respectively. The purer state can be thought of as the repetition of the corresponding state from each orientation. Hence, the physical at the physical state, the physical at the vital state, and the physical at the mental state would combine to form the purer physical. Necessarily, in the purer physical state, it is the physical that would lead. The overarching guiding ethos of such a business may be, "In fixed markets, and with fixed products, we combine and manipulate hard, physical assets to arrive at value for the organization." The primary orientation would be one of ensuring the preservation and maintenance of physical assets above others. In a particular situation, this kind of orientation would no doubt be very valuable. For instance, in the case of warfare, the protection of a country's physical assets such as boundaries and resources is paramount. At the same time, one can see that this orientation is going to provide actors of this view with a limited set of actions when confronted with change. It is not unlikely that such actors will be at a substantial disadvantage when one considers the competitive play and the very changing nature of markets. But if it were the mental part of the physical or the vital part of the physical as opposed to the physical part of the physical that leads, one can see how this would vary the practical orientation of governance. If it were the mental–physical that leads, for instance, it would be the preservation of the accumulated goodwill or brand that would be most important. This orientation would likely be very important in a situation where a corporation could uphold brand by the right tweaks, as opposed to major market-plays.

In practical reality it will unlikely be the purer state that would lead, for humans and corporations are complex entities with many different potential combinations that will interact to determine the overall practical orientation of a company. To illustrate, the three states within three orientations yield nine seed-states that can lead. Assuming many parts to an organization, the general kernel or state of each of these parts of an organization combined with kernels or states of each of the others, yields many different kinds of possible cultures.

No doubt from time to time it will be useful for a business organization to purposefully step into a certain state of being at will. In other words, given a particular challenge, is it possible to assume a mental–mental or a vital–physical or a vital–vital approach, for instance, to best respond to it? This would require that that part of being or way of being becomes active in that part of the organization that is responsible for a particular response to a particular situation. In other words, the functions of marketing, finance, research and development, or engineering, amongst others, would each require a certain kind of seed orientation in order to do justice to the nature of their required roles. But that kind of self-awareness, defined by both clarity of the seed orientation one may be holding at a particular time and the ability to change it to another seed orientation depending on the demand of a particular situation, is rare even at the level of a person, let alone a collectivity of multiple personalities that together comprise a larger sub-organization.

There is an important point to draw out here. One can perhaps see that a particular orientation, that is, physical-leading, vital-leading, or mental-leading applied at a particular time would yield the best outcome possible. But unless one were first able to become aware of these potential states of being within oneself to begin with, there is no way that a sub-organization responsible for a particular response will ever be able to create a particular way of being first. This hints at the link between the consciousness at the level of person and the corresponding organizational response. We will come back to this a little later, since this link is at the crux of the fractal model.

For our analysis the fundamental question is whether these seed-states are potentially in alignment with the sun-marked physical–vital–mental fractal. This becomes important, because if not, then we are potentially looking at many more sources of contrary and opposing fractals that ultimately lead to stagnation as opposed to progress. On the positive side, there are now many opportunities for individuals to exercise or prepare for traversing the rite of passage into a fuller and more creative individuality; only these have to be recognized.

THE BEST-RUN ORGANIZATION

In the sun-marked physical–vital–mental fractal that we are hypothesizing is embedded in the DNA of life, there is an inherent logic to the stringing together of the states in a particular sequence that culminates in a general milieu of progress. This stringing together in a manner that it is the mental that leads or that a particular process culminates in the mental state, defines progress, as already proposed. This notion of progress is at the crux of life, and those entities or organizations that are able to replicate a similar dynamic in their behavior are able to break loose of a general physical-oriented opposing fractal and arrive at an increasing expression of their identity. When this identity expresses itself, less of the opposing fractal remains, and by virtue of the fractal nature of creation, even when that creation is contained in a small space, the effect is that earth itself moves closer to becoming an earth–sun.

Like the sun all then tend to become a little more timeless, solid, vast, and self-lit. In the context of the current activity at the individual or business level, surely, this is a desirable outcome. The hurriedness of life and the orientation of decisions biased towards the short-term benefits could certainly do with an elongation of time and a more practical sense of the existence of eternity. The self-deprecating tendencies of people and the easy compromise to opportunities that waste one's energies and resources could do with a sense of solidity. The narrow frameworks and perceptions, whether at the individual or at the organizational level, could do with a sense of vastness. The easy flitting from idea to idea or trend to trend, or where the voice and call is the loudest, could do with guidance from the truth of one's self or from a state of being self-lit.

This puts into context the potential play of myriad seed-states that can be experienced by complex organizational constructs such as business organizations. It is very well to have sub-cultures and responses of many different kinds. The point is, as we mentioned in the previous sub-section, are they self-organizing to align with or even replicate in some way the sun-marked physical–vital–mental fractal? If it is many different misaligned or even random ways of being and responses that animate an organization, it will likely take on the characteristic of noise, and will, at best, allow a stepwise, labored, and, perhaps, very circuitous movement that may or may not move away from the general and seductive gravitation of the age-old physical-oriented opposing fractal. Let us, hence, examine the logic of integrating the three states for optimal running of an organization.

As we have said, an organization that is primarily physical-oriented will view the world and markets as fixed, and through leveraging existing assets will seek to maintain its position in such a playing-field. In a fixed world, this orientation will no doubt be very valuable. The world, however, is anything but fixed. Sometimes when we forget this, the circumstance will remind us of the same. Today, hence, when we consider the number of different changes underway simultaneously—from climate change to resource shortage to globalization to technological innovation amongst many others—we are again reminded that even this world, that so many are proud of now and have marked as developmentally sound, is only a temporary step in a continuous journey. To remain solely fixed in a physical orientation would yield to circumstances that themselves will likely shake the very foundation of all that is wrongly considered fixed. Myriad examples, even in the business world, of entire industries disappearing exist: typewriters, railroads, mainframes, to mention a few. For survival it becomes necessary, therefore, to combine the physical orientation with at least another. Such an orientation could be the vital. In the vital orientation, the world and markets are viewed as constantly changing. Change is dictated by application of energy. Such an orientation already allows a much higher degree of adaptability. When the goals of a business organization, hence, are sales-growth, market-growth, or other financially-led goals, the means become less important. When extrapolated, we have a situation therefore, like one we are faced with today, where other business responsibilities to society, such as stewardship of resources and corporate citizenship are foregone in the interest of a narrowly-defined self-interest. Hence, while this orientation provides energy and adaptability, it requires to be combined with another orientation—the mental orientation. Mental orientation allows deeper questioning and rationalization to enter the picture. Hence, narrowly-defined self-interest can be expanded to include larger responsibilities to society and to future generations. Also, fundamental raison d'être can be clarified, and such examination and clarification is invaluable.

From the point of view of completeness of action, therefore, it seems necessary that the three orientations combine with one another. We have arrived at this conclusion through examination of sole orientations and the lacks they would be faced with when operating individually. Let us re-look at the situation from the point of view of positives. The physical orientation is secure and is based on actions that have culminated in an organization's success to date. Current assets are a result of past success and provide a stable foundation on which future action can take place. For completeness of action, even if an organization is primarily idea-driven, or even when there were plenty of these towards the late 1990s with the birth of the Internet era, they would need to backward-integrate so as to ensure that they have a secure physical foundation. The vital orientation is driven by energy and assertiveness and allows an organization through these very devices to take most advantage of its time in the present to create its future. The mental orientation allows reason, questioning, identity, and idealism to drive organizational creation and action. One way of being complemented with another allows for a more integral, meaningful, effective, and stable action to manifest. This is summarized in Figure 3.2.

FIGURE 3.2   Logic for Integration

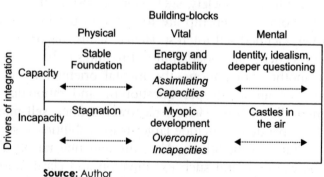

Source: Author

Without reference to the sun-marked physical–vital–mental fractal, and without reference to the effect of the fractal resident in people of business organizations, even if one were to consider business logic alone, one would still arrive at the conclusion that the most well-run organization would be mentally-led, with physical and vital orientations being subservient to it. A physical-led organization would seek to maintain the boundaries of past actions and the way of being by subsuming vital and mental capacities and capabilities, such as finances and energies of various kinds and ideas and know-how respectively, to it. This could very well lead to sub-optimal operation and likely demise in periods of rapid change. A vitally-led organization would seek to grow itself at any cost by commandeering any and all assets, and by gross rationalization of its purposes, to ensure it had the foundation and support necessary for what would very well turn out to be irrational growth. A mentally-led organization on the other hand, more than any other, would likely be led by idea or idealism, and mobilize the necessary funds and infrastructure to support it. Through leveraging higher purpose, relatively speaking, and through broader and more comprehensive questioning when it came to times of change or matters of societal context, such an organization would likely be the best run.

THE CAUSAL LINK

Let us remind ourselves that what we are trying to establish is a fractal model that ultimately illustrates quite concretely how global change is connected and in fact driven by change at the individual level. For this to be true, the fractal for progress at the individual level that has been established to be a manifestation of the ubiquitous sun-marked physical–vital–mental fractal, must similarly have its counterpart at the next significant level of organization, the business, which we have just illustrated. Further, the fundamental physical, vital, and mental building-blocks at the personal or individual level must have causal connection with the physical, vital, and mental building-blocks at the business level. Let us focus on exploring this causal connection.

If an organization is run with a physical orientation, we can predict that it will run into particular kinds of problems, and even advise that it adopts more of a vital or a mental orientation depending on the circumstances it is faced with. To briefly illustrate, in times of rapid market change, physical orientation would only allow step-wise and closed-box thinking. To be able to arrive at a creative new play that can move an organization to a new level of operation, it will be necessary to either forcibly look at expansion into new and unrelated products and markets—the vital play—or rethink raison d'être to arrive at something completely different even if it is in its existing market—the mental play. To be able to successfully execute on either of these, however, it will become necessary to dislodge or shift the current thinking and possible feelings of key leaders in an organization.

This means that at the personal level, there has to be a shift from a physical orientation to a vital or a mental orientation. Who a person is being, therefore, has to go through a change. This will have to occur at the level of both feeling and thought. If market conditions and one's historical orientation in the market has been of a particular kind, the entire thinking and feeling associated with ways of operating in that situation has to change. On the side of thought, if one believes that everything is fixed, then the likelihood of engaging in any kind of change is very low. This fundamental orientation in thought will need to undergo a shift so that markets and the world can be viewed as flexible and changing, either randomly—the vital orientation—or purposefully—the mental orientation. Similarly, the fundamental orientation in feeling will need to undergo a shift—for without the right kind of feeling driving action, action is unlikely to occur, or sub-optimal action is likely to occur. It may be the case that in the face of change one is experiencing continued inertia or complacency—primarily "physical" emotions. In such a case, to expect meaningful action is unlikely. Even if the emotional response changes to negative "vital" emotions such as anger or fear, action is possible, and the organization may shift out its current situation. The quality of the action, however, will be questionable.

But taking the linkage even further, if there is a fundamental response of feeling at the individual leader level, then corporate action will also have the texture of or tend to emanate from that level. To illustrate, if one is experiencing inertia, then what is the impetus to change the way things already are, even if repulsive? Hence, the feeling being at the physical level will tend to reinforce corporate action at that level. If there is a response of fear or anger at the individual leader level, essentially negative self-referencing flows of energy characteristic of the vital level, the corresponding corporate action will also tend to be of a similar characteristic: myopic self-referencing flows of energy at the vital level. This may manifest as lay-offs or cutting of corners so that, for instance, financial results appear positive.

Stepping back from this, the question is what kind of response is being created by leadership in the face of change? If it is a response that is driven by a belief that the world is fixed and no substantial change is possible—a physical orientation at the level of thought—and is accompanied by a mixture of inertia and fear—a physical–vital component at the level of emotion—then sure enough that is the reality, through timely and pervasive influence, that is going to assert itself in the world of that organization. Corrective action has to start at the root, and in this case, the fundamental underlying response at the level of thought and feeling that is going to determine future action in the face of the change will need to be changed. But, this individual response and its resultant effect on organizational action reinforce the strong link between an individual's orientation and resultant action in an organization. It reinforces the notion of a fractal—of a pattern repeating itself on different scales. If from the response of a "fixed world" accompanied by feelings of inertia in the face of that, the response is changed to one of "variable and purposeful world" accompanied by feelings of enthusiasm, the organization will be much better positioned for success. If the seed-fractal is changed, then the organization has a chance to go through a corresponding positive change. This notion is summarized in Figure 3.3.

FIGURE 3.3 Fractal Model Causal Link

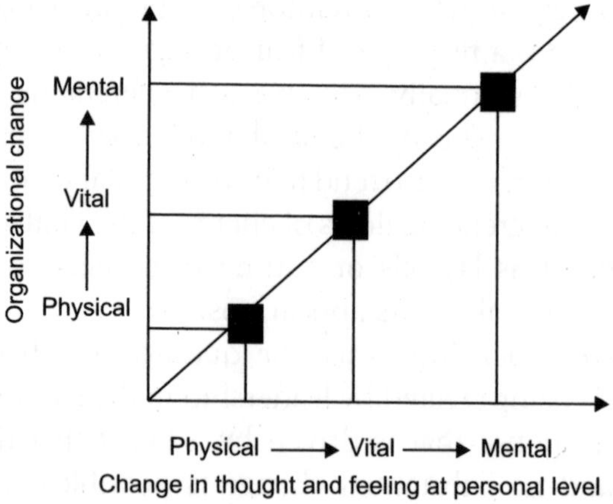

Change in thought and feeling at personal level

Source: Author

While it is the general thrust of the book to establish the case for a ubiquitous fractal by establishing the naturalness or automaticity or self-emergence of that pattern at each progressively more complex level of organization, at the same time it also shows the link between one level and the next more complex level as we step from rung-to-rung in the Fractal Ladder as useful. This is what we have done here, and will return to a more complete examination later in the book.

SUMMARY

In this chapter, we began with an examination of what the terms physical, vital, and mental could mean in the context of the business world. We applied the physical, vital, mental lenses to each of the three terms iteratively in order to arrive at a fuller comprehension of the architecture of these terms. In some sense, this reinforces the inherent advantage of an approach of this nature. We then examined some of the complexities of combination of these individual states in the context of organizations. We considered that a large number of potential seed-states was possible, and asked the question if it is possible to step into a particular seed-state at will. This highlighted the potential link between the individual and the organization in terms of states at the level of individual influencing or even determining states at the level of organization, thus "independently" hinting at the validity of such a fractal model. Note, as stated earlier, that while our overall approach to validating a fractal model is to examine each "level" of complexity—individual, organization, system, evolution—independently, it is still of value to ensure that from a point of view of practical logic that link makes sense as we step through the sequence of levels. We then reminded ourselves of the desirable outcome of seeing or replicating the sun-marked physical–vital–mental fractal in the business world and went on to a separate examination of the logic of combining these states with the mental-leading to arrive at the optimal running of organization. The logic itself suggested that these states need to occur in the same sequence as the sun-marked fractal for the most optimum outcome thus establishing the automaticity of the fractal at the business level. We then revisited with a more concrete example the link between the individual and organizational states of being, and suggested that for organizational change to come about, the action must take place first at the root, that is, at the individual level, thereby further validating the hypothetical fractal model.

While we have focused on business at the level of individual or distinct organizations, we now need to turn our attention to the cumulative effect of business, or the next layer in the fractal model, that of economy. This is the focus of the next chapter.

4

The Economy Pattern

INTRODUCTION

So far we have hypothesized the existence of a sun-marked physical–vital–mental fractal that animates progressive life. We examined the meaning and possibility of this fractal at the level of the individual and the level of the business organization. The individual and the business organization are, in a manner of speaking, more "manageable" organizations in that they are less complicated than an entire economy, or the trajectory of development of the economy, or of a similar large system. Hence, our approach to the examination of the sun-marked fractal at these simpler levels was from the bottom-up. At the level of economy, however, we shift approaches, and begin to look at the existence of the fractal from the "top-down." In other words, we will initially focus on the evidence or existence of the same fractal at the level of economy and then begin to dissect it to make further sense of it.

In this chapter, hence, we will begin with the examination of a global economy fractal. We will then step back and ask how did it happen? That is, how did this fractal, running through the physical, vital, and mental phases, appear at the level of the economy? We will examine the nature of this fractal in greater detail, which will reveal some interesting practical characteristics. We will then begin to dissect the nature more closely to look at what the implications of what we are seeing are. Specifically, the notion of multiplicity will be examined, and in this particular case, the multiplication of "mediocrity." We will then examine the cumulative effects on the person, drawing back to our notion of a yesteryear pointing physical-oriented fractal. We will then conclude with an examination of where it is that business and the economy need to go, in light of the hypothesized fractal model that we continue to develop.

THE GLOBAL ECONOMY FRACTAL

Broadly speaking, the global economy has traversed three stages. These are the agricultural economy, the industrial economy, and more recently, the digital economy. Let us examine this more closely. The agricultural economy is primarily focused on a more physical asset—the land. Its very modus operandi has tended to be physical in nature. That is, it is all about working physically, with physical implements, to rearrange or exploit earth-based physical assets. It is all about operating with "what the eye can see." Hence, we may conclude that the focus on agriculture is really a focus on the physical phase of the global economy fractal.

More recently, over the last century, focus has shifted on industry. This focus is all about working with large flows. Its very purpose is to create large flows. Hence, there is the flow of cash leveraged to bring about flow of product. In the bargain, telecommunications flows, people flows, resource flows—which also includes energy and metal extraction, energy and metal processing and distribution—other flows of trading, flows of financial instruments of all kinds to further bring about the essential flow of product have been accelerated. In other words, the focus has been all about the "play of energies," which is characteristic of the vital phase. We can conclude, then, that the industrial phase is synonymous with the vital phase, and that by engaging in this kind of industry, the global economy has essentially traversed a vital phase.

Currently, we have entered into the digital economy. The late 1990s saw the birth of the Internet era. It was idealism of sharing information, of transcending traditional silos that gave birth to the Internet. Subsequently, there were a number of radical ideas, relatively speaking, that gave birth to new companies. For instance, it was possible to bring a virtual library and bookshop with millions of titles into one's living room, or to conduct all financial transactions on the computer. The focus of this phase of the economy was much more on ideas. In other words, the focus has been on the mental phase.

The global economy, hence, appears to have gone through the physical, vital, and mental phases automatically. It is not that someone decided that now a majority of business activity will transition from one emphasis to another. There is a level of self-organization here that, as the term suggests, happened by itself. It is not that the mental phase appeared first, followed by the physical, and then the vital. The phases appeared in the same sequence as the sun-marked physical–vital–mental fractal. The automaticity of this is important, for it suggests that if progress is to happen, the logic of the sun-marked physical–vital–mental fractal that we are suggesting is imprinted in the very DNA of life, must be followed.

THE GLOBAL ECONOMY FRACTAL AND PROGRESS

The question is: Has progress happened? To answer this, we will need to refer to the elements of the ubiquitous fractal itself. Many will say that progress is going to depend upon the base orientation that actors within a system have. Let us follow this line of thought. If the general orientation is "physical," then the most important element for actors is going to be preservation of the past world. In this case, the dynamics of past markets, past communities, past roles, is what will be viewed as the standard. Change that breaks these boundaries will be threatening and, in the final analysis, will not be viewed as progress, but more likely as chaos.

If the general orientation is "vital," the most important element for actors in the system is going to be constant change marked by the aggrandizement of one's own individuality or organization. So long as the chief actors of that system are benefiting, and in a vital world, this will necessarily be the few who are strong or energetic enough to impose their worldviews, it will be deemed that progress has happened. Chief actors are perhaps the captains of industry, the autocrats or self-proclaiming elite of government, and those few others who support the enriching of the few by pocketing riches in the bargain themselves.

If the general orientation is "mental," then progress is going to be determined by acceptance of some commonly-accepted or vied for utopia. Notion of utopia may compete with notion of utopia. But as long as the spirit of true questioning remains alive and more of an attempt is made to arrive at a universal sense of utopia, this will be deemed as progress.

Using these notions of progress, in whose context may we have progressed? Certainly not for any who have the physical orientation. For the world as we know it seems to change its basic bearings from day to day. And reality of yesterday continues to be further shattered as any day leads to a new day. For those who have the vital orientation, they have certainly progressed, for the few are getting richer at the expense of the earth and many communities and people around the world, and what is more, the commonly accepted notion of progress is generally synonymous with the notion of business development. That is, so long as business is developing, and so long as all are playing their parts to progress world business in general, constituents or actors are considered useful. For those who have the mental orientation, there has likely never, in the last few decades, and even perhaps centuries, been any generalized and deep enough questioning as to the purpose of it all. On the contrary, there has been acceptance of a way of being that has been successfully imposed by those in power. Hence, even from a mental orientation, progress has not really happened.

If progress is only true as defined by a vital orientation, is it true progress? This question necessarily leads us into the idea of a fractal within a fractal. By definition, a fractal is a pattern that repeats itself on a different scale. Hence, this kind of dissection should be natural when fractals are used as a lens to study any phenomenon. When we assess, hence, that the global economy has gone through the pattern as depicted by the sun-marked physical–vital–mental fractal, and if our hypothesis about progress being synonymous with this proposed ubiquitous fractal is true, then we must conclude that any movement through the physical, vital, and mental phases in that particular order must necessarily result in progress. How can this be true though when the earth, communities, and many individual people have paid an unfair price for that progression? The progress can be seen as progress if we consider that the current movement is happening within a single, larger physical, vital, or mental phase, and is in fact the ubiquitous fractal applied to that overarching phase that is thereby pushing the boundaries of that phase. In other words, the current global economy fractal that has progressed through the agricultural–industrial–digital phases is a manifestation of the sun-marked physical–vital–mental fractal applied to, or within the limits of a larger, overarching vital phase of the economy. This idea of a fractal within a fractal is captured in Figure 4.1.

FIGURE 4.1   The Global Economy Fractal

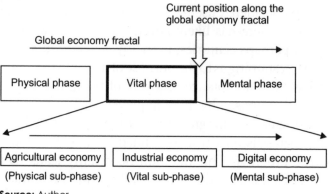

Source: Author

The true nature of the current global economy is vital. Within that our increasing digital focus, the indication of the culmination of a physical–vital–mental movement, suggests that we are approaching the limit of the vital economy. Let us probe this further. Approaching the limit would suggest that there is going to be a general breakdown of the accepted order or way of doing things. Without going into a detailed analysis at this point, are we approaching a general possible breakdown? Several global indicators would seem to suggest this. Witness the recent financial crises with the utter breakdown of the global financial system. Banks and numerous other prestigious financial institutions the world over have declared bankruptcy. National economies have declared recession and some even suggest they are on the verge of depression. Witness further, in the decades preceding these recent events that even though monetary wealth had been increasing for regional and the global economy as a whole, the happiness of people was reported to be deteriorating.

Further, climate change has become a major issue and if not adequately addressed within a prescribed time-frame, will reportedly lead to major catastrophes on many different fronts. Finally, the earth is in general in a reality termed as "overshoot." That is, earth's ability to sustainably generate natural resources is short of demand for these resources and this gap appears to be growing daily. Analysis suggests that these major trends are a result of human action, and further, a result of business-as-usual. This phenomenon will be explored in further detail in subsequent chapters. The point is, our business mindset and actions seems to be pushing us to the limit of the "business" way of being. Hence, it certainly appears that we are approaching the boundaries of a certain phase.

This can be reaffirmed by examination of the progressive formation of the modern institution of the corporation. Through the last couple of centuries, the modern corporation has been accorded many of the rights of a human being, for example, the right to buy property, the right to protection under the law, but not perhaps equal accountability and responsibility to society. A human being has rights, but is also strictly accountable before the law. The same cannot be said about corporations.[1] Corporations, for example, have been granted limited liability. Couple this with the rapidity with which financial assets can be transferred to parts of the world where a corporation does not operate, or which are tax havens, and many large corporations exist in a reality where they can become centers of incredible flows of various kinds, without equal responsibility for the impact of those flows.[2]

This is very unlike the situation of a person who under most circumstances is under scrutiny of the law where (s)he lives. In other words, the modern day global corporation is the quintessential vital animal. Its birth is vital in nature and, therefore, the reality and the world it has reinforced around itself by dint of fractal pressure is necessarily vital. It is not surprising that the economy is bumping into limits, as is evidenced by some of the trends we just reviewed. If its birth has been of a vital kind, we know, by applying the logic of the sun-marked physical–vital–mental fractal, that if it does not complete the movement to incorporate and in fact be led by the mental component, it will stagnate. In other words, given the possible overarching reality of a ubiquitous sun-marked physical–vital–mental fractal and the necessity of progress embedded in this fundamental movement, and the fact that as per our analysis, the global economy fractal is already at the limit of the vital phase, it is a foregone conclusion that the modern-day institution of business must either radically transform or will be replaced by something of an entirely different nature. We will have more to say about this in subsequent chapters.

Let us return to the further examination of the modern-day global economy fractal. We have suggested that the global economy is fundamentally in the vital phase, and within that, has traversed the physical and vital sub-phases, and has recently entered into the mental sub-phase. We asserted that this movement, even though of a primarily vital nature, is progressive because it is pushing us against limits of the vital phase. In fact, the general issue can be restated in terms of an initiation rite. The general obstacles we see around us now can be thought of as the manifestation of a contrary fractal, in that its nature is not to yield to the mental control, but is likely to continue forever with the untransformed vital dynamics, and has, therefore, resulted in the construction of a passage-way through which we must pass to breakthrough to the other side. This becomes our rite of passage—for it means that a very different way of being has to emerge in order to overcome the challenges of today.

DEGREES OF FREEDOM

Let us also pause here and examine the notion of the degrees of freedom afforded to the primary actors in the vital phase. From a vital standpoint, the physical or agricultural economy allowed some fulfillment of the characteristic vital goals of self-assertion, conquest, self-aggrandizement, and flows of energy even if of a random nature, often at any cost. But this was not enough. To create slave labor or even slave traffic from one region of the world to another, so that requisite amounts of sugar or cocoa or spices could be cultivated, and feed a global industry that in turn fed the taste buds of some target populations, that in turn enriched the captains of commerce and other favored elite, simply did not afford enough vital satisfaction. In fact, all it had done from the vital point of view was perhaps whet the appetite of the chief actors of this system. This focus on the agricultural or physical phase allows its actors only a limited amount of "degrees of freedom." They were bound by "what the eye can see"—by current markets, current products, existing target customers, and existing strategies. There was a need to push the limit into another way of increasing vital satisfaction. This way was provided with the birth of the more complex machine.

It is not that the birth of the complex machine was a bad thing. It was just that the general milieu of the time controlled by opportunistic vital actors was such that its appropriation to drive the engines of industry and the consequent birth of the industrial economy was perhaps inevitable. This entry into the vital phase of the vital economy provided many more degrees of freedom to its actors—it became a "play of energies." Product, market, customer, were no longer bound. Thought was appropriated to dream new strategies, processes, devices to continue to feed the vital kernels of these actors.

The general populace had clearly not developed enough of the sense of identity and uniqueness to even challenge what was happening. If this had happened, perhaps now there would be no need for a more formidable rite of passage. Unfortunately this was not to be the case. For by now, the general sense that all exists for business and that business is the only way for the world to progress had been embedded in just about any and every institution. The vital phase of the vital economy fully fulfilled its purpose in this regard, and the sense that reality is nothing other than a vital play in a vital world became as though deeply ingrained.

And now this general belief was so formidable that even when the Internet was born, due mainly to entirely non-commercial reasons, its possibilities were like the emergence of the complex machine before it quickly appropriated to push the global economy into the digital or mental phase. In other words, the general vital milieu had now a new set of channels and methods to continue to push its basic vital agenda. Barriers to trading and facilitating flows of all kinds broke down. Product and more products were more easily put in the hands of consumers. Instant gratification was being pushed to its limits. Demand for resources, intensification of production processes, of course expedited the push against limits. While there is, no doubt, great promise and many good things that have simultaneously emerged with the birth of the Internet (these will be put into context in a subsequent chapter) the point is that it has also provided the chief actors of a vital phase the icing on the cake so as to speak, that pushes their degrees of freedom to a new level. Figure 4.2 summarizes the notion of increasing degrees of freedom as orientation shifts.

This notion of increasing degrees of freedom also sheds light on why, logically, it would make sense for an economy to move from a primarily physical to a vital and then on to

FIGURE 4.2   Increasing Degrees of Freedom

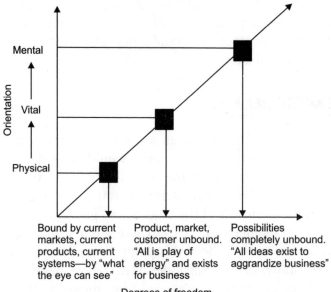

| Bound by current markets, current products, current systems—by "what the eye can see" | Product, market, customer unbound. "All is play of energy" and exists for business | Possibilities completely unbound. "All ideas exist to aggrandize business" |

Degrees of freedom

Source: Author

a mental orientation. For such movement accords the chief actors added capabilities—in the form of increased physical, vital, and mental powers—to more fully achieve what they want to. At the same time, and this is no doubt not in the active consciousness of the chief actors, it expedites the movement toward the limits of a particular system, increases the need for potentially heroic efforts to address the resulting challenges, to thereby facilitate the birth of the next phase in the ubiquitous fractal.

In our hypothetical model, the DNA of life is embedded with the implicit need of progress as charted out by the sun-marked physical–vital–mental fractal. This means that all nature's constructs, whether the individual, the organization, the economy, or any other construct that we may not have considered yet, are pushed to transcend their limits so that they reach that mental stage of sincere questioning. While that may seem like the end point of the journey given where we are currently placed, in itself, it is likely only a starting point to a whole set of new possibilities. This will be explored in greater detail later.

THE MULTIPLIER EFFECT

We have stated that it makes sense if chief actors have a vital orientation that the economy would have developed the way it has—through the agricultural, industrial, and beginnings of the digital phase—because this movement brings into the hands of the chief actors greater satisfaction of the overarching vital goals. There are a few important observations to be made at this point. First, the chief actors are still individual personalities. The whole development of levels or organization removed from them—in this case the level of corporation, and then further, the level of the economy—takes on the characteristics and hue of the seed-patterns or kernels resident in these chief actors. Certain vital tendencies, as it were, exist to fulfill their realities, as we hypothesized earlier. These tendencies determine the nature and characteristic of the business organization created. Through fractal pressure, this nature and characteristic reinforces itself by influencing and drawing other entities into its orbit. An entire business organization with this fundamental characteristic, in turn, becomes a multiplier of the same effect—a more complex dynamo in a manner of speaking, to both broadcast and receive, and thereby further imprint or reinforce this general vital tendency on the nature of life. When a whole host or business organizations all exist for the same purpose—vital self-aggrandizement—the resultant fractal is formidable. Mental components will easily find themselves subdued to this general atmosphere, and the reinforcement of cycle upon cycle creates an economy that in itself is like its actors, chiefly vital in nature.

As discussed in Chapter 2 (The Person Pattern), at the individual level, tendencies compete with tendencies, and through careful observation and effort it is more easily possible to bring certain tendencies that are arrested in their fractal movement into the light, so as to speak, to make them progress or somehow even to dissolve them. When, however, a business organization of a certain nature is created, it has already taken on an aura of impersonality. That is, its characteristic and culture now seem to exist on their own, and do not lend themselves to the opportunity of being changed or transformed or dissolved so easily. Push out another level of general organization to the level of the economy at this stage, and the essential character by the same logic will be far more difficult to change. Media, personalities, larger societal norms will have been imbued by the general character of the economy, and if another way of being is suggested, it will be viewed as non-traditional or non-conforming or generally destructive to the established goals of life, or even perhaps as heresy, depending upon how deeply embedded other actors in the system are to the now established way of things.

In this general development of layer of organizational complexity laid upon layer of organizational complexity, it is as though veil has been placed upon veil, and as citizens we have forgotten that the root of what exists "out there"—with the problems of decreasing happiness, or widening inequality, or systemic resource shortage, or climate change, or whatever else may manifest—exists within ourselves as tendencies or kernels or seed-patterns that through force of creativity and fractal pressure must create what they have been brought into existence to create. These levels of increasing impersonality, in effect, imbibe the removed levels of organization with all the strength of a yesteryear-pointing and contrary fractals that in effect acts to prolong its reign and its incomplete way of being. Our own biases and traumas and inconsistencies and ignorance creates kernels within ourselves that do the very work they were created to do, and result in massive and progressively removed levels of organization, culminating in the general tendency and thought of cultures and society, and become formidable obstacles or challenges that in the final analysis are the very material against which we have to battle in order to assert our nascent and true individuality. Recall that the general habits and ignorance are not truly us, but tendencies that have manifested in us because they exist in the environment and are part of the ubiquitous yesteryear pointing fractal that seeks to prolong its own reign. That individuality, in fact, as we have already stated finds expression and its right to be when it has successfully encountered the demons of its own creation, and surpassed them with new creations and a deeper reality of being that becomes a creative force in its own right.

We know that the global economy fractal, as we have stated, at the boundary of the vital level tending toward the mental, is therefore none other than the expression of who we are in the way of our being. When we speak of the business world and the economy needing to move to the next level in the sun-marked physical–vital–mental fractal, it is therefore we as individuals who first need to complete that same journey. The organizations we create and the society we have created are indices of our own personalities. If we are bumping into global limits by this logic, it must be the reality that we are bumping against limits of who we are being in the first place. If we have to reinterpret or reform business organization and the global economy, its nature will have to find its key in the shift in nature that we ourselves have to go through. Figure 4.3 captures this idea.

FIGURE 4.3 The Multiplier Effect

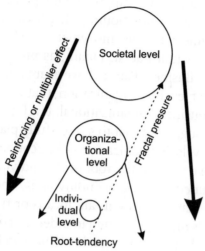

Source: Author

SUMMARY

We began this chapter with an examination of the manifestation of the ubiquitous fractal at the level of the economy. We then questioned whether this manifestation spelt progress and discovered that what we were seeing at the level of the global economy in fact was a fractal within a fractal. The birth of the digital economy was the mental sub-phase in an overarching vital phase. We concluded that indeed progress was happening, and it was the nature of the progress to push to limits even the depravity of a certain way of being. We examined the notion of degrees of freedom, and suggested that logically even, without considering a possible fractal model that in any case would lead us to reinterpret our entire way of looking at things, it made complete sense for an organization to want and need to traverse the physical, vital, and mental phases for its own fulfillment. In so doing, however, along with the apparent progress, the shortcoming of the approach would come more into relief, and if noticed and acted upon, would potentially lead to an entire new way of functioning, that it can be predicted, would be in line with the movement of the sun-marked physical–vital–mental fractal. Finally, as previously done in Chapter 3 (The Business Pattern), we examined the causality linking different levels of organization, that is, the individual level to the business organizational level to the level of economy, and suggested that to successfully plan or envision where larger levels of organization—the economy—must go, one would have to go to the root or the individual level. We further concluded that the economy as is, and the myriad organizations that comprise it, are means or rites of passage that individuals must go through in order to arrive at a deeper and truer possibility of what can be. What can be is hinted at in the possibilities of the sun-marked physical–vital–mental fractal that of course exists in the DNA of life.

5

The System Pattern

INTRODUCTION

So far our essential line of development has been to observe instances of the ubiquitous sun-marked physical–vital–mental fractal at progressively more complex levels of organization. We started at the level of the person, progressed to the level of the business organization, and in the previous chapter, studied the level of the economy. It was found that the fundamental building-blocks of the ubiquitous fractal, which we derived from observation of the phases of the day in the mutual earth–sun dance, shed insight into the structure and essential operations of those levels. When strung together or combined in the same sequence as the sun-marked fractal, we have observed that the conditions for progress at that level logically and even automatically come into being, as would be predicted by the fractal model we are in process of developing. When strung together in different sequences however, opposing fractals come into being. Through fractal pressure, the opposing fractals tend to reinforce their reality and hence the status quo. Opposing them, however, can become a rite of passage by which the sun-marked sequence and hence truer identity can manifest in oneself, in the construct exhibiting the opposing fractal, and through fractal pressure, in larger and larger levels of organization. We also observed, as we would expect in a fractal model of this nature, that there is a causal link between a building block or fractal at one level and the nature of the next level.

Earlier, we had stated that if there is validity to the ubiquitous fractal, that is, to the physical–vital–mental sequence, it must be evident regardless of where we look. So far we have looked at a person, a business organization, and the global economy as a whole. We have found that this sequence manifests when there is progress at that level of organization. We chose these instances because they are each manifestations of progressively more complex organizations. In other words, they represent different scales in organizational complexity. Recall, that a fractal is a self-similar pattern that repeats itself on a different scale. Now, however, we want to cast a wider net and begin to study instances of the same sun-marked fractal in different areas of life. While there are, no doubt, more examples than we can possibly enumerate here, for illustrative purposes we will choose a few samples from diverse areas. These will illustrate how the ubiquitous fractal pattern is abroad in many areas of the "system."

In particular, we look at a couple of system-wide economy related fractals—the digital economy fractal and the energy industry fractal. We will then look at a couple of system-wide fractals related to global politics—the balance of global power fractal, and the exchange rate fractal. We will also look at a couple of fractals related to science-based system of thought—the physical fractal and the biomimicral fractal. Finally, we will look at two system-wide general fractals—the organizational design fractal and the fractal of progress.

SYSTEM-WIDE ECONOMY RELATED FRACTALS

Let us start the broader approach by focusing on the mental sub-phase of the vital phase of the global economy fractal, the digital economy, to see whether the same pattern has manifested itself here. It is interesting to note that broadly speaking, even the digital economy has been characterized by three distinct phases. When it first came into being, entities indulged in what we can in retrospect call brochure-ware. That is, they simply took what they had available in existing media or brochures and replicated that onto web pages. In other words, they took what "the eye could see" and put it onto the new "media" as is. Fundamentally, the business model remained the same, it continued with the status quo. In other words, brochure-ware exemplified the physical phase of our hypothesized ubiquitous physical–vital–mental fractal.

Some more adventurous entities then experimented with the second phase of the digital economy, which we can call e-Commerce. In this phase, selected business processes were transferred onto the Internet. The most common being the customer-ordering and customer-fulfilment processes. That is, selected business flows, aimed at increasing selected financial results, were mapped onto the Internet. This is none other than a vital dynamic. Hence, e-Commerce can be thought of as the vital phase of the digital economy.

Some entities went even a step further and invented/ reinvented or reconfigured themselves to highlight fundamental Internet-based characteristics as the basis of their business models. Hence, such characteristics as global ubiquity, 24 × 7 presence, disaggregation whereby entities can focus on what they do best and partner with select entities that have core competencies in other areas, amongst other characteristics, became the basis for reinventing the business model. Such re-conception is none other than a mental-level dynamic. The re-conceptualization can be thought of as the mental phase of the digital economy.

We see that the physical–vital–mental phases have manifested in that very sequence in the digital economy. It is not that there was collusion or the stepping back of players to decide the time for the next phase in the sequence to happen. It happened by itself because it made sense to do so and because the degrees of freedom of the players involved were increased when the physical tended to the vital, and when the vital tended to the mental. Perhaps we can even say that it happened because of the pressure of the ubiquitous sun-marked physical–vital–mental fractal that is embedded in the DNA of life, which seeks for instruments to continue to push forward the dials of progress. We will return to the example of the digital economy and the notion of progress in more detail in the next chapter. This progression of the digital economy fractal depicting the relationship with increasing degrees of freedom is captured in Figure 5.1.

FIGURE 5.1   The Digital Economy Fractal

Progression of digital economy

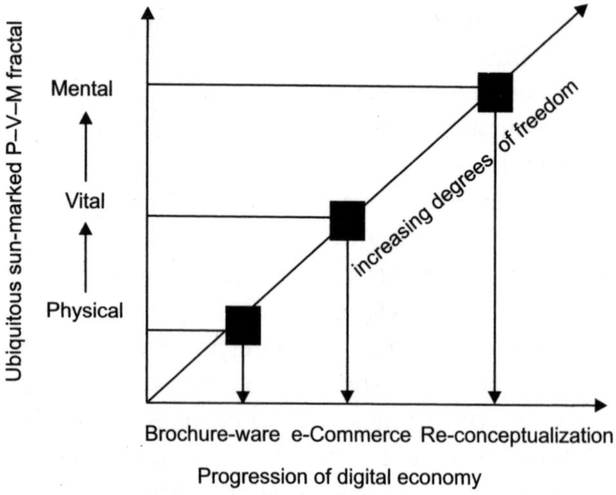

Source: Author

Let us also examine the appearance of the physical–vital–mental fractal in one of the most highlighted areas of today—energy. Here too, the energy industry is displaying movement through the same three phases. For decades, the focus of energy availability has been primarily through extraction—the primary source of our energy has been carbon-based through oil and gas extracted from the earth. Let us understand this orientation in a little more detail. In this orientation, the world is viewed as fixed: our source of energy is oil and gas, and these have always provided our energy needs, and will continue doing so. Such notions as the imminence of peak oil, that states that petroleum production will decline at the point where the rate of global petroleum extraction reaches a maximum,[1] are imaginary or no cause for worry because if it exists, it exists in the indefinite future. Further, a carbon-based energy world is what our world is and nothing can change that now or in the future. In the worst case, if we run out of points of extraction under our existing control, we will extend that control into other regions of the world, or perhaps even into other worlds if need be. This is a purely physical orientation to life, in which the notion of what has been is what will continue to be.

In the face of an increasing acceptance of peak oil and the increasing reality of climate change—a direct result of our obstinate insistence on a way of being that has outlived its utility—there has been a growing shift to maximize existing flows of extracted energy. Without fundamentally altering the source, we are gravitating toward a mindset of allowing the extracted energy to remain in existence longer through changing the way it flows and the way it is used. That is, we have begun altering devices and the way energy flow takes place through pipes, so as to prolong existing flow. This orientation on prolonging or maximizing existing flows is none other than the vital orientation. Ideally, the vital orientation should have existed right from the beginning. But the apparent abundance of extracted energy has not necessitated the movement from the physical to the vital phase of the energy fractal. Actors have been satisfied in staying where they are and it is only when the limits of a certain orientation are reached that the more progressive amongst the actors are willing to alter their orientation, thereby, also increasing their own degrees of freedom and their ability to become instruments for the underlying sun-marked physical–vital–mental fractal.

However, this fractal story does not end here. The most progressive amongst the actors have taken a leap into alternative non carbon-based energies. There is an out-of-the-box thinking on how energies from other sources can be made practically available and utilizable, and on what a non carbon-based economy may look like. This kind of thinking is representative of the mental dynamic and marks the early transition into the mental phase of the energy industry fractal. A point to be made is that if the ubiquitous sun-marked physical–vital–mental fractal is a reality, and it certainly seems like it may be, though we will discuss this in detail in the next chapter, we already know what shifts people need to make within themselves to facilitate and remain ahead of what seems like an inevitable path on the part of the larger energy fractal. The leaders, whether of this fractal or any other that is discussed, will be those who can make the physical–vital–mental journey in themselves.

The energy industry fractal and its relationship with increasing degrees of freedom is depicted in Figure 5.2.

SYSTEM-WIDE GLOBAL POLITICS FRACTALS

Let us first consider the fractal of relatively recent global politics. Here, too, we see a shift from the physical to the vital to the mental phase. However, like the fractal for the global economy, the active and overarching phase is currently at the vital level, and within that we have traversed the fractal within

FIGURE 5.2   The Energy Industry Fractal

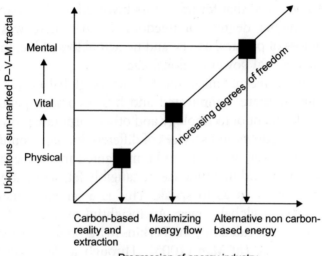

Progression of energy industry

Source: Author

a fractal, through the physical–vital–mental sub-phases. Hence, in the earlier 20th century, politics was marked by physical prowess and threat. World Wars I and II epitomized this physical orientation in which politics was largely about a display of physical powers—armies, weapons—and involved threat to physical boundaries by virtue of physical armies. Balance between global powers was a result of such displays of physical powers. This was the physical phase of the global political fractal.

Post World War II, politics was not so much about the actual physical powers possessed by a country, but by the fear-factor involved were the physical powers to be unleashed. Fear, hence, was the motivating lever. In the Cold War, it was the threat and fear of possible nuclear attack that maintained the balance between global powers. The confrontation was not physical; it was based on emotion and, therefore, based on self-referencing flows. This is a vital dynamic. Hence, for practical purposes, politics shifted to a primarily vital phase. It is to be noted that for the actors involved, such dynamics offered higher degrees of freedom, in that there was no actual loss of physical assets, and no actual loss of life, to yet maintain actual power in global affairs.

In more recent times, the balance of global power has become far more complicated and has become dependent on development of technology and other corporate prowess. Through products and services of different kinds, a country's culture and way of being can be implanted in another part of the world, and its influence be tangibly felt without even lifting a finger so as to speak. This is a far more mental orientation to global power. An insightful overview of this approach is provided by John Perkins in his book, *Confessions of an Economic Hit Man* (2005). Through a clever idea, a whole new way of being can exercise its influence in another part of the world. The promise of local or national business development can cause local governments to yield to other governments. In such a manner global power is maintained. This orientation to maintaining global power allows its actors an even higher degree of freedom. In that, development and the exercise of novel ideas, as opposed to physical assets or vital ploys and masquerades, can alter the global balance of power. This relationship is captured in Figure 5.3.

Let us look at another manifestation of global power and politics in the setting of global exchange rates. At the start of this exchange rate fractal, the method for setting global currency rates was purely physical. The amount of gold—a concrete and practically timeless physical asset—a country had determined the strength of a country's currency. This is a purely physical orientation.

At some point, there was a more sophisticated strategic approach that was thought out. The relative vivacity and effective strength of a country's activities in the global

FIGURE 5.3 The Global Politics Fractal

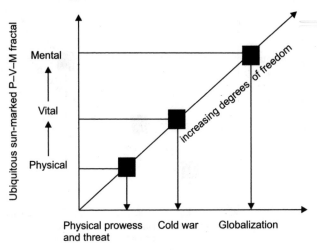

Progression of global politics

Source: Author

arena, measured through demand and supply of a country's currency, was being used to determine its currency rate. This is a mental orientation and of course offers actors involved much higher degrees of freedom in that creativity and unleashing of a country's powers can literally overnight alter the demand for its assets.

In reality, we are today at some kind of middle ground between the planned ideal and the gold standards of the past. Hence, today, currency rates are for practical purposes set by the balance of power. This is the vital play. Even though it should really be the real-time creativity of a country that determines the demand for its assets, the negotiation between presidents with side deals of all sorts is much more effective in doing so at the moment. Nonetheless, the trajectory is the same. We have the physical level gold standards of the past, the vital level negotiations and side deals of the present, and the mental level real-time creativity of a country of the future. This is summarized in Figure 5.4.

FIGURE 5.4   The Exchange Rate Fractal

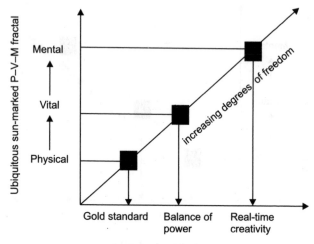

Progression of exchange rate

Source: Author

FRACTALS RELATED TO SCIENCE-BASED SYSTEMS OF THOUGHT

We will begin by looking at the fractal for physics. For centuries, physics has had a primarily physical orientation. Atoms were thought of as being the indestructible building-blocks of all existence. These building-blocks were thought of as acting according to fixed laws. All matter was composed of these fundamental building-blocks. If one understands the nature of these laws and the nature of the atoms, then everything is known regardless of differences in time or in space. That is, regardless of how short or long or how slow or fast time moves, or how minute or vast space itself becomes, the laws even if understood within a certain time and space, would apply inevitably as the same laws in all time and space. This orientation is physical in nature and perhaps is known as the atomic view of nature.

In time, it yielded to the quantum view of nature. This, as we will see, is more of a vital orientation. In the quantum view, the fundamental building-block is no more a fixed and indestructible unit—the atom—but a dual wave particle that changes its nature based on observation of an actor. Waves become particles, and particles become other particles. There is a spontaneous flow that seems to accompany the fundamental notion of reality. This notion of flow is essentially vital in nature.

It is not that there is a grand purpose or a unifying theme or a teleological underpinning to reality. That would imply a mental orientation, and is perhaps where physics is tending to move currently. Hence, the active trajectory has been physical to vital to the beginnings of mental. The same physical–vital–mental fractal is revealing itself. This is captured in Figure 5.5.

While the physics fractal spans a few centuries, let us turn our attention to an entire field that is only decades old, that of biomimicry. Biomimicry is concerned with the

FIGURE 5.5 The Physics Fractal

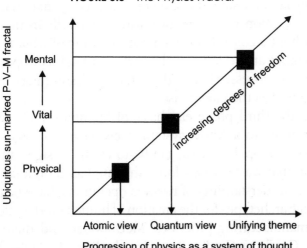

Progression of physics as a system of thought

Source: Author

design of product and process through emulating nature.[2] In some respect, this is centuries old and some of the wisest, most sustainable man-made designs through the centuries have been a result of mimicking nature. In recent decades, however, it is interesting to note that this very field has gone through three active phases. In the first phase, there has been an imitation of the form and function of nature. That is, form and function, the outer physical aspect of nature has been mimicked. An example is as in the velcro strip which imitates the form and function of a plant in nature. This approach to product and process design is clearly at the physical phase.

Biomimicry then began to emulate process as opposed to form, that is, the focus shifted to the way nature manufactures product. The emphasis is not on "why," but more on "what." Hence, for example, nature's approach to manufacturing insulin was emulated by an understanding of the process by which this happens. The same agents and the same process as those occurring in nature were then emulated at manufacturing scale. This imitation of process, without getting into the how and the why, without fully understanding the larger system question of how product manufactured in this fashion might interact with other cells in the body, or without a comprehensive understanding of what is really happening at the level of the cell, is a vital as opposed to a mental process. Hence, this phase of biomimicry can be thought of as the vital phase.

In the third phase emphasis of biomimicry has shifted much more to a whole systems view. Hence, designs such as closed-loop lifecycles, cradle-to-cradle design, and the notion that waste equals food, that are based on a far more holistic understanding of nature's operations, have begun to become archetypes for the creation of human product designs and manufacturing processes. McDonough and Braungart's book *Cradle to Cradle: Remaking the Way We Make Things*

(2002) is an insightful exploration into this approach. This is clearly at the mental level where deeper and more elaborate system design is understood and then becomes the basis for not just replicating, as in the physical and vital phases, but of the formulation of design principles that are then leveraged in the creation of product and process that have hitherto never appeared in nature. Hence, we find the same physical-vital-mental sequence repeated in the specialized field of biomimicry. This sequence is summarized in Figure 5.6.

FIGURE 5.6   The Biomimicry Fractal

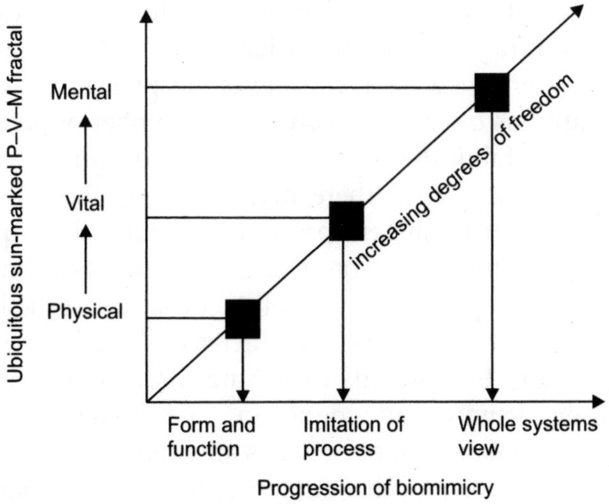

Source: Author

OTHER GENERAL FRACTALS

In organization thought, too, we see an instance of the ubiquitous fractal repeating itself. When an organization is first conceived, it is often done as a conglomeration of distinct and isolated departments. There are perhaps many ways in which these distinct departments could in fact interact with one another and operate together. It is interesting to note, however, that in most cases what emerges quite naturally is a silo mentality. Each department, unit or function views itself as independent from the others. These attitudes or biases get hardened into fact. What emerges is the physical view—the fixed view of a fixed world—which has its utility within which different departments or functions or units are able to specialize and incarnate something of the meaning of that silo more fully.

If an organization were to continue with this orientation however, increasing inefficiencies would result soon. Of necessity, the organization would need to morph into another conception of itself. As we look at the historical evolution of the modern-day organization what we find is the function of department view morphing into the process view. The organization is often re-conceived as a number of processes that exist to fulfill the stated goals of the organization. If it serves customers, then there may be a customer ordering and a customer fulfillment process. There may be a quality management process, a product design process, amongst others. These processes typically cut across established functions of departments, and increase the "flow" in the organization. Established views are broken down, and increasing activity and connection are bought into the organization. Raw material sources are linked to subsequent value-adding activities that culminate in the final product or service that the organization provides. In this respect this is a vital orientation to organizational design.

A mental orientation would necessitate the organization reconfiguring itself in real time to best allow fulfillment of what is needed to be accomplished at the moment. All moments would lead inevitably to fulfilling the raison d'être of the organization. This, hence, would be the real driver of organizational design and in the end-analysis stand as the arbiter for how an organization needed to morph in order to fulfill its purpose. It may be the case that processes become fully dynamic in nature, that is, the required process taking control as the need arises. Processes and focus become active as needed. Parts of the organization reconfigure themselves to dovetail into the needed focus areas. Note, that such an organization can only come into existence once the physical and vital stages of organizational design have been mastered. For a real time re-conception of activities of an organization require a high degree of skill and capability that the other phases allows it to develop. Hence, the organization design fractal too, appears to display a sequential movement through the physical, vital, and mental phases. This is summarized in Figure 5.7.

FIGURE 5.7 The Organizational Design Fractal

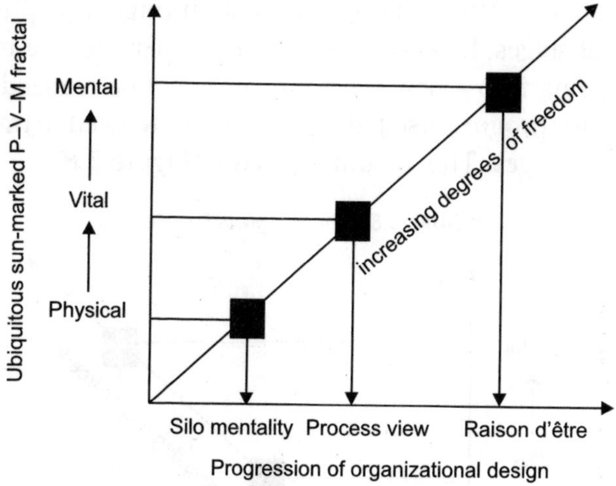

Progression of organizational design
Source: Author

Through the length of this book, it is stated that the sun-marked physical–vital–mental fractal is the fractal embedded in the DNA of life, and that pushes life to make progress. But let us independently examine the process of progress. Whether one is learning to play tennis, learning a new language, or a business is learning the ropes in a new market segment, there appears to be a common three-phased process of progress. At the first stage, there is an introduction to the elements of the new field. One learns the alphabet—the basic elements which when practised lead to mastery in the area. These basic elements each have their distinct reality and appear as independent entities that have to be assimilated into one's way of being. This focus on learning the independent and distinct elements is like passing through the physical phase of progress. The reality of the ball and its motion, the racket and its motion, and the stroke combining the two, have to be independently practised again and again. Then a phase of experimentation begins, the phase of vitality, where different combinations can be practised. Finally, this culminates into a phase of mentality, where uniqueness and truer mastery can manifest. Without first passing through the physical and vital stages, however, the reason for playing, the reason for entering into a new segment can never be realized. The process for progress itself, therefore, seems to need to traverse the three stages. This is summarized in Figure 5.8.

FIGURE 5.8   The Progress Fractal

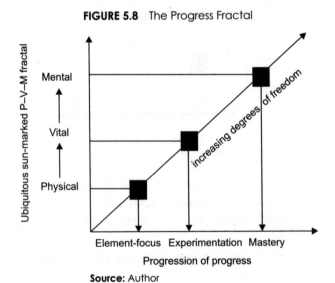

Source: Author

SUMMARY

In every system-related fractal discussed, the trajectory of progress is determined by the physical–vital–mental sequence of phases. It is not that the majority of actors move automatically from one to another. Rather, it is the leaders who make the move. We can hypothesize that they were able to make the move because within themselves it is the mental orientation that is far more active than the vital or physical orientations, or that they worked to make this the reality of who they were being. The rest of the actors followed, as a natural act of survival, precisely because it is the mental level that affords many more degrees of freedom. The natural tendencies, the traditions of the hour, are no doubt backward-pointing. Against this general milieu, it is our hypothesis that the break from the past to the future offered the various protagonists of the aforementioned fractals a chance to further strengthen their individualities. Their uniqueness and way of being was reflected in the general breakthroughs that manifested in the shifting of phases of the fractals themselves. It was the rush of this experience, of incarnating something of who they really are, that in itself becomes the draw for completing or pushing the respective fractal journeys. We can further hypothesize that this inherent draw, this urge to complete the fractal journeys originates from the reality of the ubiquitous sun-marked physical–vital–mental fractal that has embedded itself in the DNA of life.

In this chapter we have thus examined general fractals that occur at the level of the system. This examination completes our general examination at progressively larger and more complex levels of organization. In the next chapter we will turn our attention to the process of evolution, and then step back to examine the fractal model and its validity.

6

The Evolution Pattern

INTRODUCTION

So far we have focused on several rungs of a potentially single ladder consisting of progressively more complex and encompassing instances of organization. Interpretation and clarity with respect to dynamics of these rungs was afforded by hypothesizing a seed-pattern prevalent in the mutual earth–sun dance. This seed-pattern revealed the building-blocks for each rung on the ladder. Many different creations are possible, and we hypothesized that the stringing together of the building-blocks in a particular sequence will determine the nature of the creation or creations at that particular rung. We also hypothesized that the rungs are part of a single ladder, if and only if the building-blocks are sequenced to replicate the sun-marked physical–vital–mental pattern at each subsequent rung all the way till the highest rung we can conceive—a level that transcends efforts by the human species. This has to be the case if we are talking about a single ladder that connects the person-level to such a level. That is, this hypothesis has validity only if we see the physical–vital–mental pattern prevalent at a level where human beings have had no possible influence over the existence of this pattern. This would prove, from a logical point of view, that indeed the hypothesized seed-pattern that we started out with exists in the context of a larger, beyond human creation, such as the mutual earth–sun dance.

If this were the case, this fractal ladder, then conceivably forms part of a special imprint that is in a manner of speaking a ubiquitous blueprint for progress. We examined the person rung, the business rung, the economy rung, and several instances of the "system" rung. In other words, we have examined successive levels of human creativity and found that indeed progress at each of these levels is determined by the particular sequencing of building-blocks as embedded in the sun-marked physical–vital–mental fractal. That is, where this sequencing is not repeated, we do not see a progressive creation, but rather a status quo or even a destructive creation. Now, we step beyond systems of human creativity to examine the canvass of nature. Does this same imprint of progress manifest itself in the DNA of nature? If so, as we have suggested, this opens us to a wholly different context and interpretation of the fractal ladder.

In this chapter, we will examine if the physical–vital–mental pattern similarly exists in nature. If so, we will further apply the same architecture of a day—the physical, vital, and mental phases that complete its sense—to gain further insight into the physical, vital, and mental phases that must have appeared in nature. We will examine the implications of this progressive imprint in nature. We will, in particular, examine the vast output of the last century in the context of this progressive imprint. This also leads to an interesting reinterpretation of history and geography. From the vantage point which we will have gained we will also examine the meaning of the earth–sun dance in more detail. We will reserve the next chapter, however, for re-examining the rungs and context of a potential fractal ladder and for beginning to shed a different light on the established systems and other possibilities of human creativity.

THE PHYSICAL PHASE OF THE EVOLUTION FRACTAL

Getting right to the key point, in a nutshell, records of evolution on earth have indeed revealed a progressive manifestation. In very broad terms, a purely "physical" creation characterized by inanimate matter, yielded to a progressively more active "vital" creation characterized by many different life forms, that in turn yielded to a progressively more active "mental" creation characterized first by simple mental capability in animal form, and then by relatively more complex mental capability in human form.

Let us examine this journey in more detail. In the beginning, there were purely material elements of the likes of rock, minerals, and water. This perhaps can be thought of as the physical sub-phase of the physical phase of the evolution fractal. Figure 6.1 sheds light on this breakdown.

This sub-phase is characterized by the creation of visible material elements. There is no movement and no activity between the material elements. These base materials house many different atomic and molecular configurations that manifest in different color and texture and substance. These then become the basis for a more progressive creation. This initial state of stability can itself be thought of as being the result of the physical–vital–mental fractal and as the starting point for a new physical–vital–mental fractal. In a fractal model, such an analysis, leveraging recursion is natural.

In the case where the physical sub-phase of the physical level is the result of the application of a physical–vital–mental fractal, the starting point must have been a universe of atomic particles (see Figure 6.1). This initial state of atomic particle can be thought of as the physical sub–sub-phase in the physical sub-phase. These atomic particles are then fused together, likely under intense temperatures that may have characterized the nature of existence eons ago. This fusing

FIGURE 6.1 The Physical Phase of the Evolution Fractal

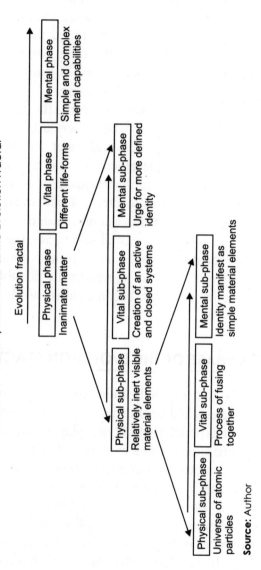

Evolution fractal

Physical phase	Vital phase	Mental phase
Inanimate matter	Different life-forms	Simple and complex mental capabilities

Physical sub-phase	Vital sub-phase	Mental sub-phase
Relatively inert visible material elements	Creation of an active and closed systems	Urge for more defined identity

Physical sub-phase	Vital sub-phase	Mental sub-phase
Universe of atomic particles	Process of fusing together	Identity manifest as simple material elements

Source: Author

together can be thought of as the vital sub–sub-phase in the physical sub-phase. When all the flowing and fusing is done, and when atomic particles have exercised their energies to form new and more elaborate structures, what results is a final physical identity of various forms of matter, the mental sub–sub-phase in the physical sub-phase.

This then is the new starting point, the physical sub-phase in the physical phase, where there are different base elements—the rocks, minerals, and water. In the vital sub-phase, the geographical placement of these base elements is rearranged, whether through earthquake or wind or storm or action of primeval fire, to create a landscape in which interaction of basic elements in a continual and closed system becomes the reality. In the mental sub-phase, the urge for a more defined identity surfaces, and a fundamental yearning to more fully express and to be, amidst the possibility of the interaction of the elements, becomes alive, as also depicted in Figure 6.1.

THE VITAL PHASE OF THE EVOLUTION FRACTAL

This yearning, this need to be more fully alive expresses itself in simple single-celled organisms. This is the start of life, of a much vaster experimentation, of a play of myriad energies, of the vital phase in nature's evolution. In other words, this basis of autonomous cellular activity represents the physical sub-phase of this vital phase of the evolution fractal. Figure 6.2 depicts this along with other developments.

At the culmination of this sub-phase, cells have perhaps learned a number of important basic functions: assimilation of sunlight and other basic nutrients from their environments, processing of these nutrients to accommodate a more complex set of basic activities such as locomotion, elimination of un-needed bi-products, alteration of genetic material

FIGURE 6.2 The Vital Phase of the Evolution Fractal

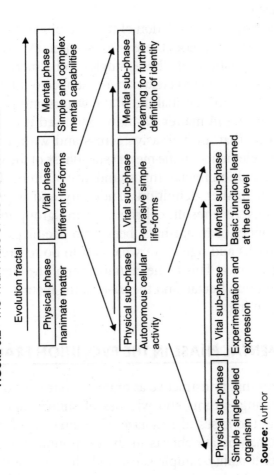

Source: Author

to accommodate new and valuable impulses, creation of different chemicals and substances that manifest in different physical features and functions, most optimal processes for sub-division and combination with other types of cells, amongst others.

The physical foundation of the vital phase has been laid. In the vital sub-phase, there is expression, experimentation and combination of these single and emerging multi-cellular organisms to create an abundance of plant life and even very simple animal life in the waters and on the land. The yearning in matter has now expressed itself in simple life forms that are pervasive across and within the initial material elements. In the mental sub-phase of the vital phase of the evolution fractal, this abundance of simple life yearns for even further definition of identity and expression of possibility. As a result, collectivities and group intelligence form. Ants live in ant-hills, bees form bee-hives, and birds fly in packs and figure out what best to do to prolong their collective lives. This is the culmination of the vital phase in the evolution fractal, and the basis of the mental level in the evolution fractal.

THE MENTAL PHASE IN THE EVOLUTION FRACTAL[1]

Thought that is instinctive as opposed to reasoned is already manifesting. Grunts and whistles of animals and birds are forming the bases of language. Coordination of hand with eye to manipulate objects in the environment is becoming more of a reality. Simple cause-and-effect relationships and logic are beginning to manifest themselves. This can be thought of as the physical sub-phase in the mental phase of the evolution fractal. Figure 6.3 depicts this along with the other developments at the mental level.

FIGURE 6.3 The Mental Phase of the Evolution Fractal

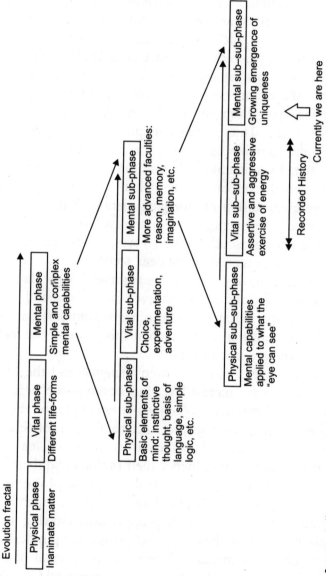

Source: Author

This development takes place using "what the eye can see" as the laboratory. Everything is applied simply to external objects. The physical sub-phase thus occurs in the physical context. Animal life applies simple physical orientation, mental-level dynamics to enhance basic life functions.

An ape now chooses to stand upright and seeks to explore the realms beyond the forest and trees. Choice, or disengagement from the herd mentality, is beginning to surface more. Thus begins the phase of more conscious manipulation of life and environment to further differentiate one's self. Experimentation more forcefully combines with basic mental-level capabilities, all in the pursuit of more complete expression of emerging identity. This is the vital sub-phase of the mental phase of the evolution fractal. Some walking apes go south, some go west, some live in caves, some near the water, some eat deer, some eat nuts, some sing at the end of the day, some dance at the end of the day, some kill with rocks, and some discover fire. At the end of this phase, the ape, perhaps, has become the common man. This marks the transition to the mental sub-phase of the mental phase of the evolution fractal.

Reason, logic, memory, even imagination—the fundamental basics for mental-level functioning—are beginning to manifest themselves. When we began exploring the sun-marked physical–vital–mental fractal at the level of person in Chapter 2, we discussed the mental orientations that a person can have that would influence their outlook and their lives. This is the material of the mental sub-phase of the mental phase of the evolution fractal drawn out over a much longer stretch of time. At first humans apply their growing mental capabilities to what the eye can see. This is the physical sub-sub-phase of the mental sub-phase of the mental phase of the evolution fractal. Possibility is an incremental function of what has already been achieved. Even that possibility cannot transcend certain limits inherent in what has already been created through eons of history. The past defines the future. Material reality is the basis which has established laws which when known, everything is known. The human being is a material being. Expression and mentality have arisen as means to prolong this material basis and to protect and incrementally enhance possibility within reasonable limits. This physical sub–sub-phase of the mental sub-phase of the mental phase of the evolution fractal perhaps marks our distant past, of the beginnings of history which, perhaps, we have lost track of or have not even considered when we consider the progression of history. This is approximately speaking, for who knows what level of sub-fractals journeying through the respective physical–vital–mental realms had to be pursued to make the shifts that would endure and to be followed by the vital sub–sub-phase of the mental sub-phase of the mental-level fractal.

The vital sub–sub-phase was likely marked by the need for assertive and even aggressive exercise of growing energies, in the interest of further expression of identity. Identity, however, was synonymous with experiencing a range of emotions and narrower self-building thoughts and actions of various kinds. I would opine, given many of the global challenges that we are facing on a simultaneous basis, that we are now beginning the transition from the vital sub–sub-phase to the mental sub–sub-phase of the mental sub-phase of the mental phase of the evolution fractal. I would opine that all recorded history is only the imperfect recording of our journey through this vital sub–sub-phase. (Both these opinions are depicted in the lower right corner of Figure 6.3 by respective arrows.) Further light can be shed on this by considering the physical–vital–mental fractal that animated this sub–sub-phase. I would opine that the human species has yet to become the true mental being. Perhaps the next thousand years is all about this.

TRANSITION FROM THE VITAL SUB–SUB-PHASE TO THE MENTAL SUB–SUB-PHASE

The point is that even when we consider the canvas of nature and its evolution, we see this progression through physical, vital, and mental phases. From carbon-dating, we know that rocks existed much before any fossils, whether of plant or animal, and certainly much longer than human skeletons. We thus know for a fact that the physical preceded the vital that in turn preceded the mental. In the discussion here, we have hypothesized how each of these phases may have unfolded, using the physical–vital–mental sequence itself to shed light on each phase of the evolutionary fractal. We have an indication that history must be very old and that we are now undergoing a transition likely between the vital sub–sub-phase and the mental sub–sub phase of the mental sub–phase of the mental phase of the evolution fractal. By some preliminary estimates, linked to initial European exploration by sea to Asia and the Americas, and the consequent vital-level exploitation that proceeded in each of these regions, the transition has been in effect for perhaps two thousand years or more, and is now reaching a pinnacle as is evident by the global problems we are facing today on many different fronts. This will be discussed in detail later. A potentially two thousand year transition from one sub–sub-phase to another perhaps illuminates the expansive time-lines of history especially if one considers that a physical phase is, by definition, obstinate and long, and must exist for a much longer time than a vital or a mental phase and the transition of two thousand years we are talking about now is in the vital phase which, by its nature, is much more fluid than others that preceded it.

On a philosophical note, when we contrast what are potentially such expansive time-lines with a day any one of us may be experiencing today, replete with its overwhelming issues, we must pause, and ask, "but what will endure?" and "what would make sense were we to step into the silence in the eye of the storm?" We will come back to this later as we begin to consider some of the properties of a world that perhaps is animated by a fractal ladder of the type we seem to be uncovering now.

Ostensibly, a defining event that has signaled transition from a predominantly vital to a more mental phase, even if it be within an overarching vital phase, is the birth of the Internet and the ensuing digital economy. This event was initially the result of idealism, a decidedly mental-level dynamic. Researchers in different universities around the world were motivated to share files and research. An "open" architecture as opposed to the "closed" or "secretive" dynamics of a self-enhancing vitally-centered organism was the basis of this creation.[2] This led to the rapid growth of local networks connecting together to form a regional and finally a global network that soon came to be known as the Internet. A very different form of interaction and communication between peoples around the world had been facilitated. Web pages, e-mail, file-sharing, voice- and audio-sharing, video-sharing, though initially designed for asynchronous communication, through the increase in computing and network processing power is for all practical purposes rapidly approaching synchronous communication. This is facilitating the formation of Internet-based communities, and the more cohesive organization of softer voices, in the face of the dominant and louder vital voices of the present, that it can be argued is expediting transcendence of existing barriers and threatening dominant corporate-based power structures.

But it should also be noted, as pointed out in a previous discussion on the digital economy fractal, that the birth of the Internet and the digital economy has also facilitated the more rapid development of vital-level tendencies, and is in fact bringing the vital-level nature of the global economy to a pinnacle. For instance, facilitated by rapid digital-based asset transfer, corporations can now more easily disconnect themselves from their action, transferring their ownership, losses, and profits, from one place of the world to another, thereby becoming more elusive and much more vital in nature. Similarly, it is much easier for desire of all kinds, a decidedly vital-level dynamic, to be instantaneously fulfilled by virtue of the rapidity and immediacy of transaction offered by the Internet. In some sense, the Internet has become a magnifier of tendencies. Since the general milieu in which the Internet has grown is already vital in nature, it is the softer voices, perhaps of the future, that, relatively speaking, are magnified more and that stand out as a potential threat to deeply-embedded power structures. It is this relative shift in power from the past to the future that is of significance. When seen in context of the overarching dynamics of a fractal model, it indicates the cusp or the potential beginnings of a more progressive dynamics in line with the overall evolutionary fractal we are presently considering.

But even these softer voices need to go through the physical–vital–mental fractal to reach a more progressive culmination of their possibilities. If they go through another pattern, or simply remain at the physical level, we hypothesize that they will not reach the most progressive culmination of their possibilities. The facilitation of the softer voices through the opening up of communication can perhaps be thought of as the base materials—the physical phase in this fractal. In the vital phase, there will be many more soft voices that are heard. Different points of view will rise to the surface. Many different points of view, let us point out, are characteristic of the mental level and is no doubt a good thing. This is especially true given that at the cusp it has been a few voices, typically that of elitist vitally-driven organizations, that some would even say are the occult rulers of society that seem to be driving things. However, in the vital phase of this soft-voice fractal, it will be difficult to judge who truly represents the future and who is just expressing because expression seems to be the thing of the day. Unless this fractal can migrate to the mental level, it will likely result in little action that truly moves the needle in shifting power away from the occult or overt and elitist rulers of society.

At the end of the day, this fractal model is about connecting inner power with global change. It is about the potential of this, were certain inner conditions to be fulfilled. These inner conditions have to do with making a fractal journey within oneself so that one may break the bounds that keep one anchored to the past. It is about a deep level of questioning in which who one stands for, at the core of one's being, is allowed to come to the surface. This cannot happen unless the various tendencies that one is inundated with and constantly lives with, can begin to recede into the background, and the authenticity of one's being, that creative ability which finds effectiveness in the fractal dynamic of influence, can come to the surface. In the light of that inner authenticity, the violations that are constantly prolonged, even by many softer voices, will become clear. Then the soft-voice fractal that is also facilitated by the Internet will find its culmination in a truer mental phase. For what standard, except that of a greater and more comprehensively perceiving and guiding light, the substance of authenticity, can possibly dissect the need of many voices and discover the thing to be done, amongst the many choices that seem to be continually flung into one's being from the possibilities of life. The progression of the soft-voice fractal is summarized in Figure 6.4.

FIGURE 6.4   The Internet Soft-voice Fractal

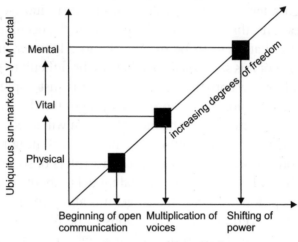

Source: Author

It is significant to note that we are currently in the extraction or vital phase of the energy fractal, which we discussed in the previous chapter. Symbolically, extraction of gas and oil is about unearthing deeply-embedded physical and vital constructs in the form of millennium old plants and animals to fuel the present. These myopic albeit energetic constructs, and what they stand for in the consciousness and outlooks they represent, have in a sense resurfaced to fuel our present. It is not surprising, therefore, that we have blind dynamics in all aspects of our global life which being of a purely physical–vital nature, cannot see beyond its own nose and is swiftly and assuredly leading us towards the end of a phase. The carbon-based economy, in this view of things, is the unearthing of an outdated way of being that needs to be worked through and resolved, that becomes a massive rite of passage, in order that we can more completely grasp the glory of the future. In this rite of passage though, repeated global crises of various kinds, ranging from social to environmental to financial, are inevitable. Culmination of a number of global fractals, including the global economy, global political, and energy fractals, that we have already discussed in previous sections, hint at the possibilities of the immediate future. These will be discussed in greater detail later in the book.

THE EARTH–SUN SYSTEM

When we view this evolution fractal from its origins of atomic particles, through inanimate matter and animate life, through birth of man, and the push to greater collaboration and reason, as made possible through the surfacing of the Internet, one must ask, who is all this for? When we viewed the fractals that were the result of human creativity, we could position the human at the center, and say that the progress is all for the good of humankind. But what when we look at this vast evolution fractal that scans the development of nature? Where was the human being in all of this? The human being is just a recent addition in the scheme of things. What is the necessity of this same pattern developing over eons and eons, and who benefits from it all?

Let us go back to the original earth–sun dance for a possible answer to this question. The earth and sun have been locked in mutual embrace since the beginning of earth-time. Some have posited that it, as most other planets in our solar system, originated from the sun. It was flung off as a ball of fire into the orbit around the sun and gradually condensed into more solid and recognizable form. Following that, it has throughout been an expression of the mutual earth–sun dance, in which its very dynamics have been determined by the nature of the dance. We had begun this book with the hypothesis that the constant spinning around its own axis, a primary movement of that dance, had embedded the three-part architecture of the day into its fibers and into its very meaning. Physical, vital, and mental phases, consequently determined the DNA of progress of the earth.

So when we come back to the question as to who has benefited from this progress, the comprehensive answer is, much more than the human. It is certainly the entire earth–sun system that has benefited, of which the human is a recent surfacing. In considering the evolution of nature on earth, it is clearly earth that has progressed. Earth has expressed the possibilities at its core, in progressively more elaborate physical, vital, and now mental garbs. It is not the structures that have emerged in the physical, vital, mental plays that have been the recipient of the progress—which is earth—that seemingly stands behind all this. Lovelock's Gaia hypothesis[3] has posited a living earth that regulates itself to ensure its longevity. But in this fractal hypothesis, we are going even further to say that the physical–vital–mental journeys gradually imbue the constructs of the earth with more of the characteristics of the sun. Earth becomes an earth–sun; there is permanence, solidity, expansiveness, and self-light that emerge as the result of successful physical–vital–mental fractal journeys. The nature of the earth changes to embody the nature of the sun in material form. The earth–sun system regulates itself to bring the energy and consciousness present in the sun into very material form using the matter of the earth. But why should this be surprising, given that earth is a portion of the sun?

Applying the fractal architecture to the earth–sun dance, we emerge with three interpretations of the earth–sun reality. In the physical interpretation, everything is "what the eye can see." This view is consistent with the view of astronomy and is most concerned with the evolution, from a material point of view, the physics, chemistry, and interaction of the earth with the sun in its material aspects. In this view, the earth is bound to the sun by laws of physics, and develops under the aegis of solar energy which becomes the basis of all chemistry on earth. The interaction of the earth and the sun sets the rhythms of days, seasons, and years.

The vital interpretation tends more, perhaps, to the views of astrology in that the apparent relative positions of celestial objects, and in this case, the relative positions of the earth and sun against the backdrop of the heavenly skies at certain times determines the nature of a vast array of earthly matters. This view is not so much about the meaning of things, as about the flows of earthly circumstances, determined by the position in relative trajectories or flows of celestial bodies. Hence, it appears to be more of a vital interpretation than anything else.

In the mental interpretation, there is an underlying and combined meaning and purpose in the interaction of the two entities. The meaning and purpose is greater and invisible and the earth–sun system is a symbol of this meaning and purpose. There is no part of this combined construct that is small or less important in this interpretation. Earth is the starting point in this eon-long journey and the earth–sun is the apparent end. The very fact that earth evolves into an earth–sun indicates that it always had the sun-potential inherent in it. In the mental interpretation of the earth–sun dance, there is also something behind the physical, vital, and mental plays and appearances, whether at the level of the person, or the organization, or the economy, or one of many systems, or of evolution on earth, that seems to be the witness and benefactor of the progress. In fact, the progress can only take place when there is a certain separation from the physical and the vital and the mental, and a realization that each of these is only a phase through which more of what exists "behind" is effectively expressing itself. We will come back to this in more detail when we consider what it means to operate in a world characterized by a fractal ladder of the type we are hopefully beginning to more concretely envision now.

The point to be noted is that as in the application of fractal architectures to various entities we have examined earlier, there is a fuller meaning and possibility inherent in the entity that surfaces and that can be grasped than in the absence of applying such fractal architecture analysis. The richness of the earth–sun construct and the possibility and meaning of it similarly comes to the surface on application of fractal architecture analysis.

SUMMARY

In this chapter, we have examined the existence of the sun-marked physical–vital–mental fractal in the progression of an eons-old nature. This brings to completion our examination of the observable rungs of existence, starting from the micro and macro fractal dynamics at the level of person, through the levels of organizations, corporation, and economy, through the various systems-level instances, culminating in the very canvas of nature. These observations have surfaced an extension to the Gaia hypothesis, to view our vaster system as a manifestation of a living earth–sun system, and left us with the question as to who is the real benefactor of such progress as made possible by the physical–vital–mental journeys. It has also left us with the question as to how fundamental dynamics of life may be re-conceived in light of a possible fractal ladder. These are questions we will begin to turn our attention to now.

7

The Fractal Ladder

INTRODUCTION

We began this book with the hypothesis that for a person to have a true impact in the world, to "become the change that one wishes to see in the world" would necessitate that the change has a way to ripple out into progressively more complex levels of organization. The change that occurred in a person would need to be able to manifest at the level of corporation, at the level of market, and at the level of system, in such a way that the nature of the change made in the person finds the pathways, or rather is able to influence the very fiber of the progressively more complex layers of organization.

This can only happen if the fiber itself is of a similar substance. To cross bounds between one type of existence and another would necessarily require some commonality in substance for this to happen. The dynamics which hold true in one kind of structure would need to find a similar substance or medium to so express itself in another kind of structure. Imagine if one were to stir water inside a pot. The stirring motion will cause waves in the water. The waves will, however, cease at the boundary of the pot, primarily because the pot is of a different substance, and responds to a different set of dynamics. If however, there were commonalty of substance between the water, the pot, and the air that surrounds it, then the waves might find expression even in the air. Only so can a dynamic begun in one medium, find expression in another.

When we think of a person, an organization, a market or a larger system, we generally conceptualize these entities as distinct, and as having different drivers and dynamics responsible for their respective functioning. In our explorations of these entities, however, we have begun to conceptualize common building blocks for each of these layers of organization, and have begun to build a language to relate and conceptualize this similarity of substance across these levels of organization. Hence, we have identified physical, vital, and mental building-blocks across each level of organization, and have observed that depending on which of these building-blocks or outlooks leads, creation at that level will be of a fundamentally different kind. Not only that, but having found that the building-blocks across levels are self-similar, we have begun to make the case that, in fact, each level is connected to another by dint of a fractal model, which in the final analysis justifies how one can "become the change that one wishes to see in the world."

This chapter is about linking the various observations we have made through the previous chapters, to establish that indeed what we live in is a physical–vital–mental fractal world. In this world there is a Fractal Ladder that connects the different levels together in a unique way. We will examine the notion of the Fractal Ladder, and begin to explore some of the implications of the existence of such a construct.

SOME FRACTAL BASICS

Let us step back for a minute. The term "fractal" has traditionally been applied to geometric shapes and implies a shape that can be split into parts that is a self-similar replica of the whole. The term "fractal" was in fact coined by Benoît Mandelbrot (1982) in 1975 and was derived from the Latin "fractus" meaning broken or fractured. Commonly appearing fractals in nature include structures such as mountain ranges, clouds, crystals, broccoli, cauliflower, fern, trees, lightning, river networks, blood vessels, amongst many others. Self-similarity in parts implies that a similar pattern occurs across progressively more minute or progressively larger scales of observation. Fractal geometry, as conceived by Mandelbrot, allowed study of real-life structures which could not be easily handled by Euclidean geometry that essentially focuses on straight lines and curves. In creating this approach tremendous insight was gained into the handling of "irregular" shapes beyond circles, squares, and triangles. This insight derived from the discovered reality that a seed-pattern, such as the broccolette in a broccoli determined the build-out of the entire structure and the final shape of the broccoli. If one does not see the seed-pattern, then the broccoli, as with so many other shapes, can occur to be quite random in nature. If however, the seed-pattern is discovered, then insight, understanding, and shaping power are placed in the hands of the discoverers. In this book, as discussed in Chapter 1, this idea is extended to more complex behavioral structures such as people, organizations, and markets as a whole.

Just as the seed-pattern in the broccoli or other fractal occurring in nature determines the final shape, so too, seed-patterns in our outlooks, assumptions, behaviors, at the individual level, determines the final and jagged lines of uncomfortable realities such as climate change, toxic pollution, and the range of common social depravities. The world out there is not really a world out there; it is the concrete expression of who we are within, and consequently what we have allowed ourselves to express through the array of choices we continually make through the course of the day. Often the choice, as we have discovered is dictated by a biased or stagnated physical or vital or mental outlook in a world that demands an objective and progressive physical or vital or mental outlook. By the nature of the similar physical or vital or mental medium that cuts across progressively more complex layers of organization or of life, to form "grooves" of a sort, a magnified expression of a bias is hence formed in layers apparently removed from the originating thought impulse.

Fractal reality, the repeating of a self-similar pattern across larger and larger scale, shows us how seed-patterns that live in people, manifest as the final "contradictions" so prevalent in our world today. The Fractal Ladder shows us the way out of these contradictions, to the creation of a progressive and fully sustainable world.

THE FRACTAL LADDER

We have continually drawn the difference between fractal realities and the Fractal Ladder. Fractal realities will emanate out of myriad seed-patterns that may have a random combination of the physical, vital, or mental building-blocks as the basis of their creation. The Fractal Ladder is connected by dint of a common pattern that replicates the sun-marked physical–vital–mental fractal. In other words, there is only one pattern that can create the Fractal Ladder. This has to be the case if we have observed the same pattern existing in the scale of the evolution of nature, at one end of the ladder, and the same pattern that determines progress in the individual, at the other end of the ladder. A ladder cannot be created unless each rung is similarly created. By "climbing" this fractal ladder, or making active in ourselves the pattern that will allow us to fruitfully connect one level to another, we, in a manner of speaking, can reach the vantage point where what we are creating, regardless of scale, is of the same nature as what we are hypothesizing is the DNA of progress embedded in all earth circumstance. The key to climbing the Fractal Ladder lies in using the physical–vital–mental sun-marked pattern as the step. It is only so that the change we make within, when consistent with that pattern, can have its progressive impact on layers removed from it.

We began our explorations by observation of the earth-sun dance, which for all practical purposes is older than history and more containing than geography. When viewed so, it can be thought of as setting the context for all that we experience on the earth. We observed a pattern, physical–vital–mental, that defined the structure of the day, and hypothesized that through the act of repetition, day after day, this pattern of progress was embedded into the DNA of the earth. Briefly, we could say that this is a physical rendering of the situation, based on the observable facts. If one were to consider the mental rendering of this situation, based on ideas, one may, in fact, say that the physical–vital–mental pattern was already embedded into substance, and is the pathway by which hidden identity is revealed, and that the structure of the day is such that this reality of existence is more fully brought into relief. We will come back to this interpretation later.

This is, in fact, the story of progress that observation of the different rungs of creation seems to reinforce. That means, in order for identity or the uniqueness hidden in each construct of creation to reveal itself, there must be a change from the predominantly physical to the predominantly vital to the predominantly mental outlook. This is no trivial passage, given that many other creations based on a "backward" pointing, or physical-leading, or vital-leading pattern prevail and perpetuate themselves. It requires abundance of effort to counter the many prevailing oppositions, and in so doing, something of the uniqueness inherent in each construct truly begins to manifest. This cannot but be, since the quieting of myriad and deeply lodged patterns will begin to reveal something of the light and truer substance that might exist behind the noise. This then sets into motion a new fractal that in climbing the rungs on the Fractal Ladder connects inner power with global change.

We reinforce that, of course, there is utility in passing through each of the phases of the journey in step-wise manner precisely because the capabilities developed and the experience of each phase better prepares the actor or benefactor of the journey to be a better instrument for any subsequent phase in the journey.

This sun-marked physical–vital–mental fractal is in fact the containing or contextual or seed-fractal, that fractal that transcends even our canvass of evolution. Quickly summarizing, we have found a self-similar physical–vital–mental pattern repeating itself at progressively larger or progressively smaller scale, depending on which end of the ladder we start from. Let us trace this journey once again. At the largest scale, in the result of the dance of the earth with the sun, we have the structure of a day manifesting in three distinct phases—the physical, the vital, and the mental, in this order. At the scale of the earth, we have the age-long physical–vital–mental evolution fractal, which has journeyed from inanimate matter through vast experimentation and vitality manifest in life, culminating in the mind of the human being. Each stage of the journey has brought more degrees of freedom to nature, and allowed more of her innate impulse and possibility to manifest itself. At the scale of the economy, we have traced a similar journey through the agricultural or physical economy, to the industrial or vital economy, to the digital or mental economy, recognizing each of these phases to in fact be sub-phases of an overarching vital economy. Within the vital economy, the progression through physical, vital, and mental has similarly proffered greater degrees of freedom upon the primary agents of the economy. Somewhat parallel to the scale of the economy, we looked at various instances of "system" level changes, across different systems. Hence, we looked at the digital economy fractal and the energy industry fractal, and found the same journey of progress existent in both these instances. We looked at a couple of fractals related to global politics—in particular, the balance of global power fractal and the exchange rate fractal—and there too, found the three-phased journey of progress repeating itself. We also looked at various systems of thought—physics, biomimicry, and organizational design—and there too, found the similar journey repeating itself. At the level of system, we looked at the fractal for learning and found the same phases repeated in this journey too. At the scale of corporation, we looked at the journey of a progressive organization and similarly found the three-phased journey repeating itself. At the smallest scale we looked at the person, and there too discovered that progressive action at a more micro scale and a progressive life at a more macro-scale manifests in the same three-phased journey. This journey is summarized in Figure 7.1.

This constant manifestation of a similar three-phased journey repeating itself at different scale is the definition of a fractal. Again, it is interesting to note that at each scale the three building-blocks are sufficient to define the nature of the corresponding world. Thus, it is perhaps fair to say that we live in a world that can be entirely defined by the play of physical, vital, and mental building-blocks. The progressive world, however, is marked by the physical–vital–mental journey in that sequence. And this pattern of progress, as we have seen, is universal across every scale we have examined, from the level of the person, to the level of the earth–sun system. The Fractal Ladder, hence, is a fractal for progress.

FIGURE 7.1   The Fractal Ladder

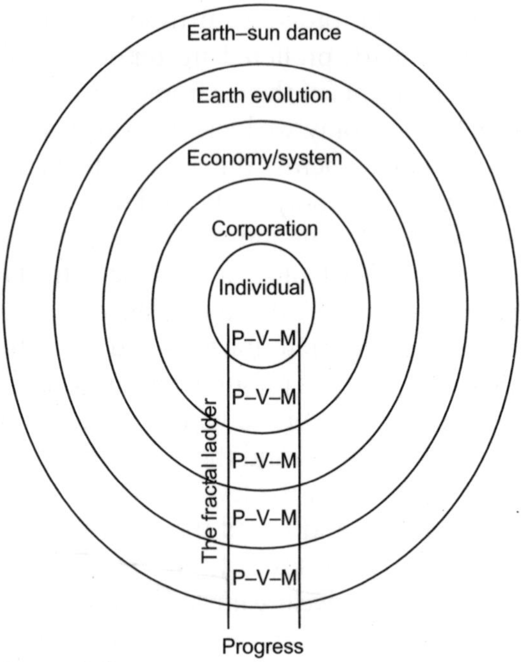

Earth–sun dance

Earth evolution

Economy/system

Corporation

Individual

P–V–M

P–V–M

P–V–M

P–V–M

P–V–M

The fractal ladder

Progress

Source: Author

PROGRESS

Progress thus appears to be an essential quality of our existence. After all, as pointed out earlier, it is not that each of the actors at the level of the economy, or in each independent system, for example, conspired to make a collective shift from the physical to the vital to the mental outlook. In fact, in spite of the major oppositions set up by myriad other fractals emanating from a vast number of habitual and even backward-pointing fractals, progress was made. Let us think about this some more. In such a milieu marked by vast opposition, for progress to be made is nothing short of a miracle. It is as though something overrides all the lack of effort, all the vested interests, all the force of habit, and in spite of all contrary tendencies, finds a way for the shift from physical to vital to mental to take place.

When we climb the fractal ladder from the bottom upward, we experience the seed-pattern of the progressive fractal as being the shift from a physical to a vital to a mental outlook at the level of a person. At the next level, we see that this shift in leaders running organizations causes those organizations to similarly change their orientation from physical to vital to mental, thereby exercising greater degrees of freedom in their environments. At yet the next level, when a collectivity of organizations makes the shift from a physical to a vital to a mental mode of operating, then a larger market or system or economy, correspondingly tends to go through a similar shift. There is, however, in our analysis, no causal link between markets and economies, and the next level up, the canvas of evolution. The time periods are too dissimilar, and yet that same shift is observed in the canvas of evolution. What does this tell us? First, the upward causality is valid only up to a certain point. Second, it is perhaps the downward causality that is universal, for the pattern is fixed in a setting beyond human history and geography and is valid in the entire field of human history and human geography. Third, while the causality is our way of interpreting observations, perhaps the fundamental take-away is not the point of causality at all, but the fact that we live in a vortex comprised of physical, vital, and mental building-blocks, in which the path of safe passage as it were, the path of progress and fulfillment, is defined by the sun-marked physical–vital–mental journey, and in following that path we open to the very character and embodiment of progress, in which new creation is possible.

It is almost as though something called Progress sits behind the vortex. It is the witness of the physical–vital–mental journey at all the different levels. It sits behind the earth–sun dance and manifests in the garb of a day. It sits behind the evolution of nature, and perhaps watches more and more complete manifestations of itself surfacing in the earth-play. It sits behind the progress of economy and system waiting for unhealthy limits to be reached so that a new and more holistic phase of progress may begin. It sits behind the development of corporations, waiting for the right actions that liberate rather than limit human possibility. It sits behind the garb of a person, leading and pushing them to embrace the difficult yet empowering sun-marked physical–vital–mental path so that true identity may manifest. Because it is so, that journey becomes possible and the human can somehow lower the myriad voices and tendencies that constantly call to it, and enter into a space where new tendencies of a very different nature can be forged and released into the world, creating entirely new and progressive fractals. This is creation; this is to own one's power; this is to begin to make a real change in the world.

The Fractal Ladder shows us that progressive creation is the same at each rung of existence. It shows us that change made in the self is of the utmost importance, for it is only so that corresponding change can be made at levels of organization progressively removed from the person. It shows us the DNA of progress, and even in climbing it, one comes face to face with a largeness that is perhaps synonymous with Progress. The fact that it exists, is reason to take notice of it and ask why it exists.

This Progress appears to have some unusual qualities. It must be present everywhere, because otherwise it would not be possible for the physical–vital–mental fractal to manifest wherever we see progress happening. It must understand and know what is happening everywhere because otherwise the appropriate shift at the appropriate time could not happen. It must be very powerful because otherwise there is no way amidst the vortex or physical, vital, and mental randomness and of a general downward or backward gravitation that the physical–vital–mental sequence could manifest. It must be connected to all human beings, otherwise the right instrument would likely not be able to appropriately make the right progress at the right time. It must be an accomplished designer because otherwise there is no way that a fractal ladder of the type we have come to observe could be etched into the frame of our lives. It must also care for us deeply because otherwise it would have left us to our own devices to sink into the obscurity from which we appear to have arisen rather than seek to lift us up into new worlds of possibility. In other words, at least in the earth–sun context, this Progress appears to be omnipresent, omniscient, omnipotent, omnicaring, and to possess other astounding qualities.

And if this is so, then what is the best way to relate to it? If it knows everything, is so powerful, is present everywhere, is connected to everyone, cares for us enough to want to etch a pathway by which we can rise from common trivialities to a mastery of life, then is it fair to say that it can hear us? Is it fair to say that it can see us, and that perhaps even it can respond to us? If so, this opens us out to a very different conception of life and possibility. We live in this Progress; the Progress lives in us. We are a result of this Progress. The Progress shapes us in its own image. This perhaps is the ultimate fractal: the seed-pattern born in Progress manifests in the earth-scene as an entity striving to embody Progress. And this Progress is not just an impartial witness; it lives here with caring and love, like a mother.

EXCEPTIONAL BEINGS

We then, are exceptional beings. We wear physical, vital, and mental garbs and possess abilities representative of these three fields of existence. But we are also something more. When we exercise the dynamic of the physical–vital–mental sun-marked fractal we partake of an essential quality of creation—we become progressive in nature. Not only that, but if in the continually successful physical–vital–mental journeying we begin to un-create all the surface dynamics of habit and commonality, and gradually enter into the silence behind the thousand voices, where we can more intimately feel our essential nature of Progress, there we may come face-to-face with the larger context that seems to be resident everywhere, and seems to be the context of our lives, and can begin to relate with it in a very different way, or even to become it. This is the great secret of our power. Even in glimpsing this, a new set of possibilities dawn.

Consider for a moment the complexity of comprehending the many tendencies, habits, mores, expectations, judgments, prejudices that each of us is continually enmeshed in. Each of these, we have said, is an uncompleted journeying of the physical–vital–mental sun-marked fractal. The habit or tendency has found some permanence because it has tended to repeat its act of stagnation. But to successfully cause the completion of the many instances of these incomplete journeys as they relate to ourselves, while perhaps not impossible, can be a mammoth task. What, however, if we were to open out these stagnated journeys to the Progress we have glimpsed? What if we were to lay the many tendencies, habits, mores, and so on, before the eye of this Progress? Would somehow the essence of what it stands for incarnate something of its essential quality or substance into the constricted entity? If what we have hypothesized is true, that this Progress is omniscient, omnipresent, omnipotent, omnicaring, and that it might be possible for us to relate to it as one even relates to a mother, then why should this type of incarnation not be possible? More than anything else, it would require a shifting in our mental outlook to make this story more of a reality. The shifting of the mental outlook is the same thing as making the sun-marked physical–vital–mental journey on this element of possible disbelief. The act of this journey is the key to climbing the Fractal Ladder and in so doing opens us out to the possibilities inherent in Progress.

On the flip-side, choosing not to progress, when this appears to be an essential quality of existence, certainly within the earth–sun context, is to consign ourselves to likely extinction. When then we look out at the vast contradictions in our world, we know that what we are facing is a tremendous choice. The contradictions are a result of seed-patterns that live in ourselves, and we must make the progress to change these seed-patterns. We must complete the many incomplete and stagnated micro-journeys that define who we are being, so that the contradictions, whether manifest in social depravities and inequities, climate change, pollution, resource exploitation, amongst others, can be transformed. This is our test as human beings. We are creators incarnate, and it is our right and responsibility to correctly exercise the tremendous powers resident in our breasts to release the stagnation in the world so that the current set of contradictions can dissolve.

SUMMARY

We started this chapter by revisiting our base fractal hypothesis. We moved on to an examination of the notion of the historical notion of the fractal. We connected together the different rungs of existence and concluded that indeed there exists a Fractal Ladder that is an instance of a fractal of progress. This Fractal Ladder has a special meaning in an otherwise random fractal world. It also puts us face-to-face with a contextual Progress that we argued must be omnipresent, omnipotent, omniscient, omnicaring, like a mother, in the context of the earth–sun dance. We further explore our relation to Progress and concluded that we are exceptional beings. As beings invested with the kind of power than can be released when one begins to climb the Fractal Ladder, we have exceptional responsibility. By owning this responsibility, we concluded that we can begin to dissolve the many contradictions that currently prevail in our world. In the following chapter we will begin to explore in more detail the properties of a fractal world.

8

Fractal Properties

INTRODUCTION

So far, we have concluded that we do indeed live in a fractal world. Structurally, there are some key characteristics of this world. The basic building-blocks of this world are of a physical, vital, or mental nature. These fundamental building-blocks determine the nature of many rungs of creation, from the personal level, to levels of entire markets or economies and systems. Further, combinations of these building-blocks form seed-patterns that are responsible for the creation of many different fractals that animate our world. Many of these fractals are backward-pointing or obstinately physical or vital in character. But there is also a fractal for progress, the Fractal Ladder, which cuts across the rungs of creation to connect micro-movements at the personal level to the very canvas of the earth–sun drama in which our lives play out.

This Fractal Ladder is a symbol of an underlying and essential quality of creation, that of Progress. Progress itself appears to be omnipresent, omniscient, omnipotent, and omnicaring, and can be entered into more conscious relation with by beginning to climb the Fractal Ladder. Climbing this Ladder equates to quieting or mastering the many contrary fractals that comprise the active substance of the many aspects of our lives. This mastery tends to push us into a space of increased silence within ourselves, the very province of Progress, from where our truer identity and more creative fractals that have the power to change our world can emerge. We are, thus, potentially exceptional beings invested with the power of creation, once we choose to climb the Fractal Ladder, rather than choose to live in the general and surrounding fractal vortex within which all our past creations and habits seem to reside.

The world hence, when viewed with this fractal lens, takes on a very different hue and dynamic. It sheds a different and more penetrating light on the many contradictions we currently live with, and on the power we are each invested with. To more fully understand this world so that we can more fully rise to overcoming the limitations we have ourselves created is an imperative. This chapter seeks to summarize and expand on some of the properties and implications of this fractal world. By so doing, hopefully, just as in the case of the fractal geometer who can now more accurately understand nature's physical symmetries and asymmetries, we too will be able to more fully understand some of our more complex symmetries and asymmetries, and be better able to exercise our power in the world.

In essence, the fractal model we have been discussing is an elaborate systems-view of the world. The state of this system is the result of the play of three essential states—physicality, vitality, mentality—in many permutations and combinations, and at many different levels. There is, however, a particular combination, characterized by the sun-marked physical–vital–mental sequence that is of particular interest to us, because when that occurs, an exceptionally progressive and creative state of the system comes into being. It is this particularly progressive state that we are most concerned with, because it is in this state that meaningful difference is born and that the system itself evolves. It is in this state that inner power can truly connect to global change. In this chapter, we will summarize and further elaborate on some of the properties of this most creative state, characterized by the pattern in the Fractal Ladder.

As has been the approach in this entire book, we will view the properties themselves, from a physical, vital, and mental outlook. The physical outlook will shed light on properties that have to do with the essential structure of this fractal-based world; the vital outlook will shed light on some of the properties that have to do with processes we can employ as actors in this world; and the mental outlook will shed light on some properties to do with ascribing meaning to actions in this world.

PHYSICAL-LEVEL PROPERTIES IN A FRACTAL LADDER-BASED WORLD

Through the course of this book we have already encountered several properties that have to do with the essential structure, or physical field, of this fractal-based world. These include properties such as universality, influence, recursion and completion. Other properties that we will further describe include evolution, matrixing, step-wise development, and feedback.

The seed-pattern in the Fractal Ladder is the sun-marked physical–vital–mental sequence. In the Fractal Ladder, it exists in each rung of creation. By knowing the intimacies of this journey or sequence, one can develop significant insight into this similar journey at another level. Thus, for example, in fully living the physical–vital–mental journey as it occurs at the personal level, replete with the nature of the phases and the transitions between the phases, one can have insight into the physical–vital–mental journey as it appears at the level of the corporation or the economy, or even in the evolution of a system of science, such as physics. Many distinct fields of experience and knowledge, which simply have no connection with one another in a linear view of the world, now share an intimacy when viewed as a manifestation of the same underlying fractal. This property is one of *universality*. The implication of this property is that knowledge of progress in one field of human endeavor can be transferred to another field, to gain at least a gut-sense for how progress may happen. Another implication is that if one does one thing really well, thereby by definition going through the sun-marked physical–vital–mental journey in the mastery of that activity or field, one should be able to not only understand but have sufficient insight into the nature of progress in many different fields.

Fractal *influence* is another property we have discussed throughout the book. This is what gives the Fractal Ladder its ladder-like quality. Fractal influence is the property by which a shift in the fractal at one level or one rung of the ladder tends to cause a corresponding shift at the next rung of the ladder. Hence, at the individual level, a shift from the vital to mental state of being in a leader may tend to cause a corresponding shift in the functioning of a corporation from the vital to mental state of being. It is to be noted, however, that this will unlikely be a one-to-one mapping. That is, it will require a certain momentum or threshold of influence before an actual shift will be seen at the subsequent level. This said, however, the fact remains that the shift itself even if emanating from one individual has put a new fractal possibility into place that, as we have discussed earlier, must have its repercussion in the scheme of things precisely because it represents a new possibility in the play of progress. It could also be the case that a shift at the higher level in the ladder can cause a corresponding shift in the lower rungs of it. Hence, if a segment of the economy shifted from a vital to a mental functioning, corporations that may be lagging would need to make this shift in order not to get marginalized. Note, however, that the shift from one phase in the fractal to the next at the level of the economy is as per our earlier arguments, made by leading companies, where the shift from the physical to the vital or from the vital to the mental outlook has already taken place in the leaders of those companies. Hence, in effect, the influence from earlier leaders is now reinforcing itself from the top-down. This kind of magnification cannot but exist in a world characterized by fractal dynamics.

Another property we have referred to is that of fractal *recursion*. That is, one should be able to apply the fractal journey to any sub-phase within a fractal. For instance, in a previous chapter we applied a fractal journey to the mental or digital phase of the global economy fractal. Hence, we found that the digital economy went through the physical, vital, and mental phases in building its possibilities. Applying recursion upward, we also concluded that the current global economy was in a vital phase, and that the agricultural, industrial, and digital phases, were all sub-phases of this overarching vital phase. This is only now hitting the boundary that could possibly lead it into a mental phase, if we were to fulfill the conditions of a successful transition. Similarly, we also applied both downward and upward recursion to the evolution fractal. Hence, we explored activity at the atomic and molecular levels through the physical–vital–mental sequence, resulting in the culmination or starting point of matter, the downward recursion, and subsequently used granular and distinct material building-blocks, in an upward recursion to explore the journey through the physical–vital–mental sequence, to arrive at the physical foundation of evolution. In this manner we saw how the recursive property of the physical–vital–mental fractal can be used to piece together likely development of entities. In a similar vein, at the level of the individual and the corporation, we have applied the physical–vital–mental sequence to shed light on what physical, vital, and mental could mean within these rungs of creation. In this case, the application of fractal recursion has been used to shed light on the structure of entities, as opposed to the process of development of entities, as in the previous examples.

Another property is that of fractal *completion*. This implies that for progress to happen, the physical–vital–mental sequence must be completed. But it also implies that the fractal wants to complete its journey. That is an essential characteristic of a journey on a rung of the Fractal Ladder. We have, of course, examined this notion in some detail throughout the book. At the personal level, for instance, if one experiences anger, a vital state, then introduction of a mental state, bringing in reason into the situation, will diffuse a potentially destructive cycle. At the level of corporation, if the leaders are consumed by greed, a vital state, then unless a higher reason for being, or thinking about the longer-term, both examples of mental states, becomes alive, the corporation could experience an Enron-like demise. In the case of a country, such as the USSR, a fixed notion of how things should be run, a physical state, resulted in its demise, perhaps because the country was not able to rise to the next level in the fractal. Hence, for progress to occur, the fractal must be completed. But what we are emphasizing here is that if the person who is experiencing anger or the company that is in the state of greed or the country that is in the physical state are on the Fractal Ladder, then completion of their respective journeys is a structural necessity—it is the nature of being on the Fractal Ladder. If these entities have no impulsion to complete the sun-marked physical–vital–mental journey, then they by definition, cannot exist on the

Fractal Ladder, but will exist in the world characterized by the fractal vortex that surrounds it.

There are other properties that shed light on the essential structure of a world characterized by the fractal-based Fractal Ladder. These include evolution, matrixing, step-wise development, and feedback.

Evolution refers to the fact that engaging in successful physical–vital–mental journeys alters the conditions within which a base journey exists. That is, the nature of the Fractal Ladder is such that all rungs of it continually go through forms of progress. This implies that the similar physical–vital–mental journeys now repeat themselves under more sophisticated conditions. Hence, for example, an organization that may have successfully risen to the mental or conceptual levels by mastering the use of information technology, say, has altered the physical and vital spaces in doing so. The physical now becomes more "intelligent," while the vital more effectively dynamic also because of the integration and application of technology. When repeated, this fractal journey starts from altered and more advanced conditions. This kind of advancement indicates that the fractal journey has been successfully completed. It also implies that an entity on the Fractal Ladder tends to go through journeys that are spiral in nature, so that each time the pattern starts over, it does so at higher initial conditions.

Matrixing refers to the condition of essential connection that exists by virtue of physical–vital–mental journeys successfully completing themselves. Take the example of an accomplished individual in the medical field. Accomplished implies that the individual likely successfully traversed the physical–vital–mental journey in their area of medical specialization. By virtue of successfully completing one such journey, the individual might now be invited to be on a policy board that regulates policy for that whole field—

this represents entry into a whole new fractal journey. The individual may also be invited to teach his or her medical knowledge to other aspiring practitioners. This similarly represents entry into an entire new fractal journey. The individual may also decide to set up a consulting firm—which again represents entry into another fractal journey. Hence, successful completion of the initial journey invited or caused connection to many other fractals each going through their own journeys. This kind of matrixing may be thought of as a device to perpetuate progress by leveraging of established insight into progress, evident by the completion of physical–vital–mental journeying, which of course, is the very nature underlying the Fractal Ladder.

Step-wise development refers to the necessity for the journeying to proceed through the independent stages of the physical, the vital, and the mental in turn, and in that order. At each stage, certain capabilities are developed that then allows the next phase to more fully leverage those capabilities to express its possibilities. But also when development at a stage has proceeded to its maximum ability within an overarching context, then the vehicle, or instrument, or actor, or urge is more ready to have the possibilities of the next phase surface. Step-wise development indicates that it is best when there is a gradual development from phase-to-phase. Were there to be another phase following the mental, that would find its fullest play if all the capacities of each of the previous phases had already been assimilated by the instrument or actor.

Feedback refers to the property by which any entity on a higher level of the Fractal Ladder will by dint of the underlying fractal pressure reinforce its raison d'être and way of being at lower levels. Often, it is the lower levels that have created the organization on the higher level. In this case, the organization at the higher level reinforces the reality by which it was created, hence engendering more of the same kind of creation.

VITAL LEVEL PROPERTIES IN A FRACTAL LADDER-BASED WORLD

Vital-level properties that shed light on processes we can employ as actors on the Fractal Ladder include intersection, flow, facilitation, and upscaling.

Intersection is a property that holds when two fractals are made to intersect with one another. There is the possibility that both fractals can move to the next rung of their respective journeys through this intersection. Consider the unfortunate destruction of the World Trade Center (WTC). The WTC can perhaps be thought of as the symbol of the global economy fractal. It was destroyed by religious fundamentalists, representative of the fractal that religion is going through. Supposedly, vitalistic, that is egoistic and self-aggrandizing dynamics, characteristic of the present phase of the global economy fractal led to oil-related aggression in the Middle East. This spurred a radical response from fundamentalists that led to the destruction of the WTC. Two vitally-centered fractals, both characterized by possibly arrested journeys, were made to collide, and in the shock, perhaps both stand a chance to progress to the next level. On one side, the destruction of the WTC leads to a deeper realization and consequent questioning of some of the methods of modern business, and perhaps forms an important stimulus to the accelerated journey of the global economy fractal. On the other side, peaceful members of a religion the world over are simultaneously led to a questioning of what religion could be made to stand for, thereby also leading to deeper questions of what it should stand for—also an important stimulus to the accelerated journey of the religion fractal.

When viewed from this lens, or through examination of this fractal property, a different and hopefully more revealing light might be shed on many conflicts the world over. The conflict should be recognized for what it is—the intersection or collision of two arrested fractals that through the collision are being given a chance to progress to the next levels in their respective journeys. Boundary conditions are always difficult, especially when the resistance to cross over to the next phase is strong. Successful completion of the respective journeys implies integration into the Fractal Ladder, a state that no doubt represents the very meaning of its existence.

Facilitation is a property that can be applied to a situation that appears to be stuck. Essentially, this implies applying a form of the physical–vital–mental fractal to the point or situation of stagnation. The physical–vital–mental pattern can be thought of as a pattern of moving from status quo—the physical—to chaos—the vital—to questioning or reforming—the mental. Applying the step of "status quo" allows one to fully grasp the current situation—the facts and the visible signs characterizing the situation. Applying the step of "chaos" facilitates movement away from the state of stagnation. The direction in which the move takes place is relatively insignificant; the point is that the movement needs to take place. This sets into motion a new energy of a different nature than that of stagnation. The final step is that of "questioning," by which a new light is shed on the situation that caused the stagnation, and possible new directions in which the energy that has been introduced through chaos, can now begin to mature.

Flow is somewhat related to facilitation and is a property by which a range of energies enter into a situation. The starting point is that of concentration on the activity at hand. If such a concentrated engagement occurs, then the physical–vital–mental fractal journey manifests itself. The beginning of the activity, whether it is reading a book, playing tennis, conversing with someone, amongst many other possibilities, may often be characterized by a state of relative resistance or inertia. This is akin to the physical level. If the activity is pursued with concentration, then a "flow" begins to arise which makes the activity easier to do. This is perhaps parallel to the vital level. Continued engagement in a concentrated manner will likely result in that same activity becoming effortless, and even perhaps in various insights related to it beginning to arise. This is akin to the mental level. This unrolling of energies is inevitable if indeed we exist in a world where progress, and progress as characterized by the physical–vital–mental sequence, is an essential underlying trait.

Upscaling refers to shifting the context or orientation from a "lower" or previous stage in the sequence to a higher or next stage in the same sequence. Shifting from a physical to a mental orientation, for example, necessitates thinking and operating in a wholly different way. From a basic outward or objective orientation, the field of relevance shifts more towards an inward or subjective orientation. Degrees of freedom associated with a situation also correspondingly changes, as does the essential psychology of the actor or instrument exercising the shift. Upscaling is a powerful approach to consider new and different possibilities in any situation.

MENTAL-LEVEL PROPERTIES IN A FRACTAL LADDER-BASED WORLD

Mental-level properties, that shed light on the meaning we can ascribe to actions in a world characterized by the Fractal Ladder, include world-wiseliness, mirroring, affirmation, integration, and uniqueness.

World-wiseliness is a property related to the mastery of several different physical–vital–mental fractals at different levels or in different arenas of life. The idea here is that the more physical–vital–mental journeys one masters, the more world-wisely one becomes. One experiences a broader range of similar phases garbed in different expressions or languages, and gains more insight into boundary conditions, and the requirements in pushing from one phase into another. A more complete sense of the mosaic underlying progress emerges and, in such a situation, one can perhaps more easily extend one's experience into previously unconsidered areas. The property of world-wiseliness is perhaps very relevant in today's world where many different ways of being are being melded together through force of convergence. World-wiseliness may also shed insight into knowing which converging fractals may prevail, because they are inherently more aligned with the imperative of progress.

Mirroring refers to the fact that regardless of where we look, what we see is a reflection of our inner state. This cannot but be true in a world characterized by a pattern repeating itself on a different scale. Seed-patterns that live in us, through force of fractal pressure, find expression and manifestation in each rung of creation. Climate change, social depravities, severe resource shortages, are outer expressions or mirror our inner states. In the Fractal Ladder nothing lies, and all events are signs of changes we must make at the level of the seed-patterns, in our essential internal outlooks and way of being, if we wish to truly change the world we have created.

Affirmation is a property that reinforces the very notion of progress. This property asserts that any successful outcome in a world characterized by the Fractal Ladder must have described the sun-marked physical–vital–mental journey. In other words, anything that is truly successful in the holistic sense must be successful because in reality it has described the seed journey that is the key to ascension on the Fractal Ladder. A simple proof of this is: Man is the master of his environment, and not the donkey or rubber plant, precisely because in man the fractal journey has reached a higher level of completion.

Integration is a property with many applications in this fractal world. In its application to leadership, for example, it implies that while leaders may exist at each phase in the fractal journey—the physical, the vital, the mental—there must be an overriding leader who is a summary of the fractal journey. That is, he must possess mastery over all levels, while being led by the very sense underlying the meaning of the Fractal Ladder. It is only such a leader who can successfully integrate and coordinate all that is going on in an organization, and yet ensure a constant freshness in direction and approach. A leader, hence, who draws inspiration solely from the vital or financial level, for example, will not be appropriate in times of major change. On the other hand, a leader who just has an intuitive sense of the underlying progress, without having mastery over the material or physical, the financial or vital, and the conceptual or mental realms, may be relatively ineffectual in getting things done.

Uniqueness emerges as fractal journeys are completed and may to some extent be defined by the particular shades, circumstances, or capacities experienced and developed along the way. Uniqueness uses the journey to emerge from the trials and tribulations of it. Crossing between or through phases often necessitates encounters with contrary fractals that forces something essential that is experiencing the journey to begin to express something of itself. Finally, there must be a shaking off of the physical, vital, and mental garbs used on the way for something to emerge from within which may use the experienced physical, vital, and mental capacities to more fully express itself.

OTHER PROPERTIES

While we have outlined several properties of a physical, vital, and mental nature, the fact is that in a world characterized by the Fractal Ladder, there is another class of properties that are equally important, if not more. The physical, vital, and mental blocks and properties that correspond to these are fundamental to an understanding of the practical dynamics of such a world. At the same time, there is a teleological sense and meaning in such a world, as is made apparent by the possible omniscience, omnipotence, omnipresent, omnicaring characteristics of Progress. In a world where there is the presence of something of this nature, there cannot but be another class of properties that have to do with the notion of relationship with such an entity. Such properties may be those of alignment with the sense of progress, or even something more active, such as aspiration for that reality of progress. They may include a laying out of current difficulties and dilemmas or a sense of surrender to such an all-knowing, all-present entity. They may include a resolve to detect fractals or sub-beings of a contrary nature and to reject their influence and reality in us, because only so does it seem that we can truly find a way onto the Fractal Ladder. Properties may include conversing with, or a love for such an omnicaring entity.

SUMMARY

The properties discussed in this chapter help us more effectively understand, relate to, and live in a world characterized by the Fractal Ladder. These properties are summarized in Figure 8.1.

FIGURE 8.1   Fractal Properties

Physical	Vital	Mental	Other
Universality	Intersection	World-wiseliness	Alignment
Influence	Flow	Mirroring	Aspiration
Recursion	Facilitation	Affirmation	Surrender
Completion	Upscaling	Integration	Rejection
Evolution		Uniqueness	Love
Matrixing			
Step-wise development			
Feedback			

Source: Author

Application of these properties should help us solve some of the difficulties and dilemmas we are currently faced with.

9

The Nature of Progress

INTRODUCTION

In Chapter 8, we posited the notion that Progress is a living entity that is all-present, all-knowing, all-caring, and all-powerful, at least within the context of the earth–sun dance. It is only so that the same physical–vital–mental pattern can repeat itself at different rungs of creation, in spite of overwhelming opposition. In this chapter, we will try and provide additional light on the nature of this Progress. In so doing, we may gain a glimpse into the way in which each rung of the Fractal Ladder, and the way in which it may progress. Such insight will help us understand how the current transition between the vital and mental phases of the global economy fractal and perhaps many other fractals that we have already surfaced might proceed.

At the start of the earth–sun dance, the earth was characterized by inanimate matter. Yet, an entire creation has proceeded from this state. This state, however, as we have begun to see, could not have been the initial state. Given that we are suggesting the presence of an all-present, all-knowing, all-powerful, all-caring Progress, it is fair to assume that this Progress has preceded all creation, and in fact, creation is a result of this Progress. It is under the aegis of Progress that creation has proceeded. This is evident from the fact that progress seems to bear one and the same signature to it, the physical–vital–mental sequence, regardless of the level of activity or organization we consider.

Progress, then, is the initial state, and in trying to isolate some relevant properties of it, we can perhaps look at manifested creation itself, since all creation has proceeded from this initial state. But why is such an examination important? Precisely because what we are aiming to do is to understand transitions and trajectories in the light of creative acts of individual power. Further, if we are saying that there is a sequence to progress, then is that sequence fully captured by the physical–vital–mental phenomenon? Or is there another state, a fourth state, perhaps, that the oft-seen and oft-repeated sequence must yield to? Because of where we currently stand in the scheme of things, and because of what we seem to have assimilated into our functioning and way of being, will Progress reveal another element to it, because we now stand more ready to embrace it and make it our own?

Not only an attempt at examining the nature of Progress can reveal this, but also, the nature of the tree is revealed in the nature of the seed. If we can better understand the seed-state from which all seems to have proceeded, then perhaps we can also gain insight into how the tree in process of growing, will continue on its journey of progress. This is important where we stand at the moment because in the flux of contradictions, a clearer guidance may help us better choose or recognize the emerging pathways towards the future. Since we do not live in the consciousness of Progress in the same way as Progress does, recognition of pathways that are resonant with Progress itself will perhaps be a useful way by which we can more successfully navigate towards the best future.

Finally, if as individuals we are successful in completing, offering, or silencing the many tendencies, which are manifestations of the uncompleted physical–vital–mental journey that is resident within us or that we live in close proximity to because they are the constant shadows of our play with life, then we must enter into a state of quietness where we come closer to Progress because all else is progressively being unmade in us. In this case, who we become in this state of creativity must be determined by the nature of Progress itself. Under such circumstances the nature of Progress more fully incarnates in our nature. This is the act of creativity. This is how our inner power manifests in the world. Because now something new and powerful from the fount of Progress itself finds expression in the world through the resultant fractals that play themselves out with the new incarnated quality in us as the seed-state.

THE FOUR QUALITIES OF PROGRESS

We have already concluded that because the same pattern of progress manifests everywhere, regardless of scale or field, that Progress must be all-present. This then must be an essential quality of Progress. We have also concluded that Progress must be all-knowing, because somehow, the right instrument is used or the right circumstance is leveraged to push towards the next stage in the physical–vital–mental sequence. We have also concluded that the act of progress, in spite of the formidable opposition that is present in all fields of endeavor from the personal to the societal levels, must require an incredible amount of power. Progress, hence, has to be all-powerful. Nothing can withstand it once it chooses that the next stage in the physical–vital–mental sequence must occur. Finally, we concluded that for such a scheme of progress and possibility to even exist in the earth–sun dance, a scheme by which each person and each level of creation can come to terms with and even discover something of their individuality and true bases of power, and further be helped along the way, indicates that Progress must be all-caring. This, then, too, is an essential quality of Progress.

These qualities are derived from a top-down view. We arrive at these qualities by applying logic to the apparent design of circumstance as they occur in the Fractal Ladder. But what if we view the situation from the bottom-up or from the point of view of what has already manifested in the earth–sun creation? Will the same qualities or further insight into their essential natures reveal themselves? For a quick answer to what has manifested we can of course refer to the Fractal Ladder itself. The building-blocks for each rung are the physical, vital, and mental states. Let us probe into the nature of these states once again since these states must also tell us something about the nature of Progress.

The physical state is characterized by all that the eye can see. It is the essential matrix of creation, the substance into which everything else manifests. It is also the index of all that has successfully manifested and that has become an essential part of life. It also reveals the incredible detail and level of perfection that has gone into the manifestation itself. Take a sweeping look at the detail, intricacy, and beauty of nature and this quality of perfection seems to arise. Take a look also at the incredible patience with which matter awaits the intervention of other dynamics, whether of vitality or mentality, and a sense of service seems to arise. This substance that is all-present seems then to be imbued with a character of detailed perfection and a quality of service. In fact, the principle of service and perfection seems to stand behind the play of the physical state. If they stand behind the physical state it is likely that they form a link between what is manifested and the seed-state from which everything has manifested.

One cannot but see a parallel between the top-down observation of Progress being all-present, and the bottom-up observation of the physical state as being all-present. One cannot but observe that there appears to be this sense of inherent service present in both. These are perhaps, therefore, parallel states with the all-presence manifesting as the physical state. But in the process of manifesting something seems also to have been left out. While omnipresence transcends barriers of time, there is mortality in physical nature. While the general forms are perpetuated, individual constructs cannot sustain themselves and decay and die in relatively short order. There seems to be a general quality of stagnation that accompanies the birth of omnipresence into finite forms. Since Progress is the ultimate designer, we must conclude that the creation of such a shadow-state is of strategic importance. Hence, while the omnipresence manifests as the physical state, it seems to almost do so from an opposite position of stagnation. Growth of possibility occurs through invoking service and perfection, the essence that stands behind the physical state. Such invocation would likely not take place unless there was a felt shortcoming. The combination of these drivers then becomes the means by which the physical state progressively embodies more of omnipresence. These relationships shed further insight into the quality of omnipresence, and are summarized in Figure 9.1.

The vital state is characterized by an essential state of energy, experiment, and adventure. It is an index of the rush of possibilities colliding with each other and reforming themselves into new possibility. It is not light of energy, but power of energy that determines outcome. The essential character, hence, seems to be that of power. In the matrix of manifested life this seems to play itself out through the trait of adventure. Each type of energy adventures towards

FIGURE 9.1 Physical-state Relationships

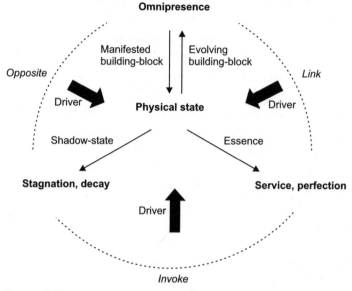

Source: Author

an expression of itself, clash and battle, and unknown outcome. But all this adventure and experiment can only take place under the aegis of power. Else, what would dare to seek fulfillment or self-destruction in such manner? The vital state, therefore, seems to be the manifested state of the quality of omnipotence. Adventure, energy, assertiveness, and growth seem to be some characteristics of its quality.

We must note, however, that though in its aspect of top-down omnipotence this essential characteristic seems to have an inevitable force and power that is ultimately irresistible, in its manifestation in the strivings of nature's constructs the power is child-like and weak, perhaps because the base through which this quality is manifesting is fragmented and strapped by limited tendencies of all kinds. As suggested, this must be a strategic decision on the part of that ultimate designer, Progress. Hence, while the omnipotence manifests as the vital state, it seems to almost do so from an opposite position of weakness. Growth of possibility occurs through invoking adventure and power, the essence, which stands behind the vital state. Such invocation would likely not take place unless there was a felt shortcoming. The combination of these drivers then becomes the means by which the vital state progressively embodies more of omnipotence. These relationships shed further insight into the quality of omnipotence, and are summarized in Figure 9.2.

The mental state is characterized by the play of the idea as the principle means of organization. While at its far rim, mentality is an index of future possibility, in its central orb, it appears to be more of an index of organizing around reason and rationalization. Increasing knowledge, consideration from many more points of view even in the organization of smaller matters—a dawning wisdom, hence, seems to be essential characteristics of its quality.

FIGURE 9.2   Vital-state Relationships

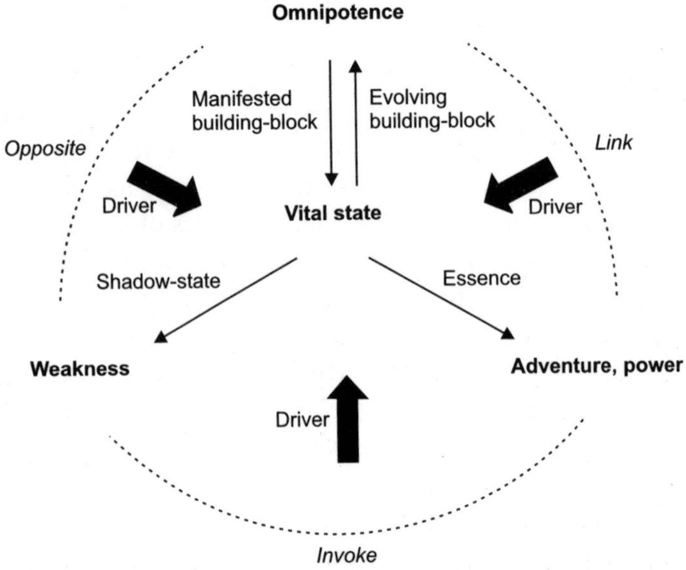

Source: Author

But in its play, it seems that while it yields insight and makes better choices possible, yet it cannot reveal the heart of knowledge. No doubt, mentality is the manifested quality of Progress' omniscience. Yet, while there is vast and intricate play and pushing of possibility in its top-down aspect, from the bottom-up, mentality is marked much more by error and ignorance. This again, must be a decision of strategic importance. Essentially, while the omniscience manifests as the mental state, it seems to almost do so from an opposite position of ignorance. Growth of possibility occurs through invoking knowledge and wisdom, the essence that stands behind the mental state. Such invocation would likely not take place unless some shortcoming was felt. The combination of these drivers then becomes the means by which the mental state progressively embodies more of omniscience. These relationships shed further insight into the quality of omniscience, and are summarized in Figure 9.3.

FIGURE 9.3 Mental-state Relationships

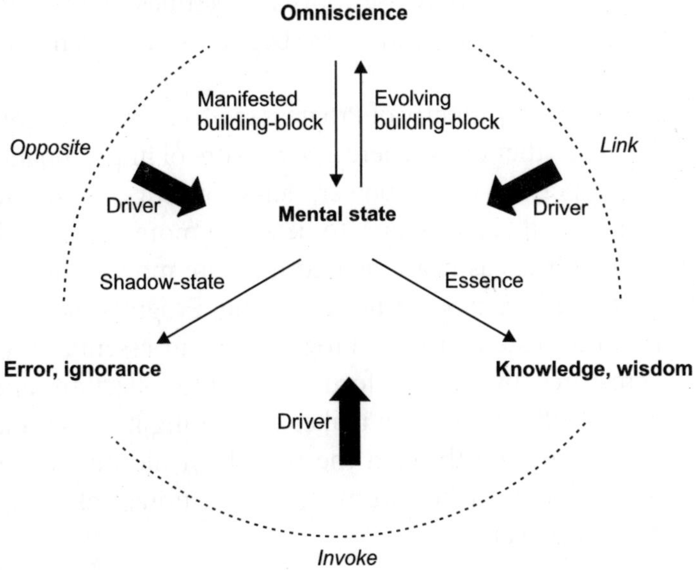

Source: Author

Let us pause for a moment and observe that the essential qualities of Progress have indeed manifested themselves in the evolution of life. The physical state is related to or is more accurately perhaps a reflection of omnipresence, the vital state a reflection of omnipotence, and the mental state a reflection of omniscience. Hence, any effort to understand the nature of Progress must be useful since it will likely give us insight into perhaps even how circumstances and events may unroll in the future.

If the physical state is related to omnipresence, the vital state to omnipotence, the mental state to omniscience, then what about the state of omnicaring? What does that relate to in practical terms? Surely it too must have a place in the scheme of things? Omnicaring is that sense of deep caring and deep love that Progress seems to have for its creation. If it did not care in this manner, it would have left the creation to sink in the obscurity of its own machinations. Instead, it has continually intervened, and even constructed this means by which we can not only rise above the pettiness of our own natures but even transform it, by beginning to ascend the Fractal Ladder.

In a sense this property of Progress seems even to be more core than the other ones. There is a measure of impersonality in the properties of all-power, all-knowledge, and all-presence. But all-caring seems to be much more personal. It perhaps manifests as heart, as that ultimate movement that gives a very different sense to everything. Progress happens because of an essential love. Progress has an essential love for its creatures, by which it forms them into reflections and images of itself. Omnicaring makes everything its child and these children grow through the travails of life into wiser, more loving beings who can more easily embrace all of life in a grasp of power.

This property is all about establishing a growing harmony. It is almost as though something significant, characterized by the heart, is growing behind the essential physical–vital–mental journey. Yet, in its growth fundamental limits of the mind itself are breaking, and leading the being into states of intuition, whereby manifested possibility can more easily touch the heart of Progress and be more securely molded by it. This is the likely fourth state, intuition. While heart seems to be behind the journeying, the next phase in an incomplete and evolving physical–vital–mental sequence seems to be that of Intuition. This is a border state that seems that it will more securely connect the top-down properties of omnipresence, omnicaring, omniscience, and omnipotence, with the bottom-up physical, vital, and mental states and make the different rungs of the Fractal Ladder more ready for the rule of heart.

INCREASING ACTION OF THE QUALITIES OF PROGRESS

This brings us to an important insight that we need to further develop. When viewed from the top-down, the essential qualities of Progress seem to act in simultaneity. Omnipresence, omnipotence, omniscience, omnicaring seem to coexist. In manifested nature, however, replete with its many fragmented creations cut off from each other by limitations of the essentially physical, vital, or still-evolving mental outlooks or some combinations of each, only some aspects of the qualities of Progress and certainly incomplete combinations of them can find expression. Hence, thinking of the physical, vital, and mental states as fields of possibility, it seems that each field progressively allows more of the four identified qualities of Progress to act simultaneously and more fully. This is depicted in Figure 9.4.

FIGURE 9.4 Coexistence of the Qualities of Progress

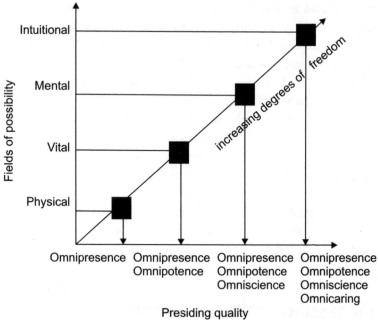

Source: Author

At the physical end of the spectrum, possibility manifests in fixed grooves. The essential expression is of the past, of what has already been brought into the manifestation. In such a matrix, the more dynamic, light-filled, and loving aspects of omnipotence, omniscience, and omnicaring, respectively, act more behind the surface in whatever way they can, precisely because the means for their overt action and way of being has not still been adequately brought out. The physical field is still too rigid, inert, and obscure to allow any meaningful expression of these possibilities. Hence, while it appears that the omnipresence aspect of Progress presides over the physical field, the omnipotence, omniscience, and omnicaring aspects are quite hidden.

In the vital stage, energies and dynamism have infused the physical, and the very physical–vital conglomerate now allows many more possibilities to manifest. While it is perhaps the omnipotence aspect of Progress that presides over this conglomerate, the substance of the field is still not malleable enough perhaps to allow the possibilities resident in omniscience and omnicaring to meaningfully manifest. Even, of course, omnipotence, given the nature of the vital field, can only appear as a reflection of itself.

At the mental level, the essential field has been even further altered to allow a more advanced play, relatively speaking, characteristic of a more intense reflection of omnipresence, omnipotence, and omniscience. These essential qualities of Progress can shape possibility, and uniqueness and identity can more meaningfully manifest.

But still, these fields have more of a bottom-up quality. They are still too tied to physicality and the backward-look. With the advent of the fourth state, intuition, however, there is now a more direct action from the essential nature of Progress, and its four qualities will likely find far more meaningful expression. Further, there will likely be a higher degree of simultaneity in their action, more akin to the essential quality of their unfettered top-down action.

APPLICATION OF THE PHYSICAL–VITAL–MENTAL FRACTAL TO PROGRESS

When we began to identify the essential traits of each of the four qualities of Progress in their interactions in the earth-play, we had suggested that service and perfection were the observed nature of omnipresence; adventure and power were the observed nature of the quality of omnipotence; knowledge and wisdom the observed nature of the quality of omniscience; and harmony the observed nature of the quality of omnicaring. While omnipresence, omnipotence, omniscience, and omnicaring can appear to be very abstract terms, Service, Adventure, Knowledge, and Harmony[1] seem to be much more practical terms and certainly easier to grasp. While omnipresence, omnipotence, omniscience, omnicaring can be thought of as end-goals in the evolution of the Fractal Ladder, Service, Adventure, Knowledge, Harmony can be thought of as the presiding motive forces under which the Fractal Ladder has been constructed, and by which it more immediately progresses.

It is interesting to note that through the analysis we have just conducted we have essentially applied the physical–vital–mental fractal to the very nature of Progress. In its physical aspect, that which we see around us manifest as each rung of the Fractal Ladder, appears as the physical, vital, mental, and intuitional states. In its vital aspect, the link state which is leading through experimentation and expression, it appears as Service, Adventure, Knowledge, and Harmony. In its mental aspect, that which is its hidden meaning and identity, appears as the states of omnipresence, omnipotence, omniscience, and omnicaring. In other words, Service, Adventure, Knowledge, and Harmony are secret names behind the operation of the Fractal Ladder. We shall examine their role more closely in the next chapters when we consider alternative bases to our current vital foundation of business and leadership. The most secret names behind the Fractal Ladder are certainly omnipresence, omnipotence, omniscience, and omnicaring. This is what the Fractal Ladder must have the potential to transform into some time in the distant future.

This architecture of the Fractal Ladder resulting from the application of the physical–vital–mental fractal is summarized in Figure 9.5.

FIGURE 9.5 Architecture of the Fractal Ladder

	Omnipresence	Omnipotence	Omniscience	Omnicaring
Meaning				
Drivers	Service and Perfection	Adventure and Power	Knowledge and Wisdom	Harmony
Building-blocks	Physical	Vital	Mental	Intuitional

M-state (identity) ⇧

V-state (link state) ⇧

P-state (manifested nature)

Source: Author

Through the action of intuition, it is possible that rigidities in the fundamental building-blocks can be reduced. This is inevitable, since action of intuition, by definition, means that the fundamental building-blocks are themselves completing their fractal journeys, since intuition is the fourth state, beyond the mental. As a result, the physical, vital, and mental building-blocks, more easily admitting of the unfettered qualities of Progress, of which in our analyses they are reflected or appear as shadow-states, can begin to admit of a different mode of operation. Hence, the rigidity, obscurity, inertia, dullness, and opposition to progress that mark the shadow side of the physical, might more easily begin to give way to their opposites. The egoism, desires, demands, vanity, anger, fear, aggressiveness, jealousy, amongst other shadow-states of the vital, might similarly also begin to give way to their opposites. The fixed notions, beliefs, constructions, narrow ideas, and noise that mark the shadow side of the mental, might also begin to give way to their opposites. As a result the physical, vital, and mental fields will begin to go through a progressive transformation. These fields will become more capable of incarnating qualities of Progress, and of allowing a higher degree of simultaneous action of each of the four qualities to take place.

If the very building-blocks of each rung of the Fractal Ladder go through such a transformation, then imagine what may happen to the creation on each rung, and to the Fractal Ladder itself. Opposition to the fractal journeys will diminish and they will be completed far more rapidly. Fractal influence, completion, universality, recursion, matrixing, evolution, step-wise development, and feedback will become more pervasive and the very structure of the Fractal Ladder will evolve with rapidity. More fruitful experimentation and adventuring will take place as the fractal qualities of intersection, flow, facilitation, and upscaling find more and more avenues to be expressed. The very meaning of individuality will change as world-wiseliness, mirroring, affirmation, integration, and uniqueness become more prevalent. As a result, the fourth state, intuition, will find forms and circumstances much more malleable to its influence, thereby even further opening out the essential structure of the Fractal Ladder to the secret names that stand behind it. The exercise of alignment, aspiration, surrender, rejection, and love will increase and constructs will open and manifest in their very natures the essential motive forces of Service, Adventure, Knowledge, and Harmony. The bases of individuals, or corporations, of society, of all manner of systems, of the very notion of leadership, will change from within, proceeding now on a multi-dimensional platform of holism as opposed to the long experienced one-dimensional platform of exploitation. Progress itself will more openly manifest in all the workings of the Fractal Ladder.

In the Mandukya Upanishad[2] there is reference to the four states of AUM. "A" is the waking state where there is consciousness of the form of things. This is akin to the consciousness of the physical, vital, and mental building-blocks, the physical or P-state in the emerging scheme of the Fractal Ladder. "U" is the Dream State where there is consciousness of the play of principles behind forms. This play of principles can be thought of as the motive forces of Service and Perfection, Adventure and Power, Knowledge and Wisdom, and Harmony, the vital or V-state in the emerging scheme of the Fractal Ladder. "M" is the sleep state, the consciousness of the principles themselves. These principles can be thought of as omnipresence, omnipotence, omniscience, omnicaring, the M-state in the emerging scheme of the Fractal Ladder. The combination of A, U, M, forming AUM, is the transcendent state, the witness, that which is everywhere, and which manifests past, present, and future.

The stringing together of P, V, M results in the emergence of Progress, that witness state, that is similarly present everywhere, and is the seed-state of the Fractal Ladder. If this analogy holds, then the seed-fractal of the Fractal Ladder, that is, Progress, is none other than that revered and ever-present mystic syllable that promises to be the ultimate secret behind all manifestation, AUM. Let us consider this more deeply. AUM in its visible manifestation is the physical, the vital, and the mental. For the physical is the form of things, the vital is the play of possibilities seeking for expression, and the mental is the idea or principles themselves. Hence, not only the Fractal Ladder in its three aspects represents AUM, but each of the rungs which string the physical, the vital, and the mental together, also represents AUM. In other words the Fractal Ladder as a whole, each of the rungs on the Fractal Ladder, and therefore every type of progressive organization from a person to entire systems is also a manifestation of AUM. This then stands as the most secret nature of Progress. This analogy is depicted in Figure 9.6.

SUMMARY

We began this chapter with a restatement of the top-down qualities of Progress. We then looked at the Fractal Ladder, as the instance of manifested Progress, to surface from the bottom-up other insights into the nature of the qualities of Progress. We arrived at the notion of deeper principles or motive forces, Service and Perfection, Adventure and Power, Knowledge and Wisdom, and Harmony, behind the established building-blocks of the Fractal Ladder. We then considered the coexistence of the essential qualities of Progress as they preside over the fields of possibility set up by the physical, vital, mental, and intuitional building-blocks.

FIGURE 9.6 AUM and the Fractal Ladder

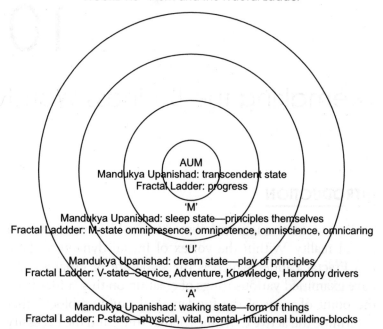

AUM
Mandukya Upanishad: transcendent state
Fractal Ladder: progress

'M'
Mandukya Upanishad: sleep state—principles themselves
Fractal Laddder: M-state omnipresence, omnipotence, omniscience, omnicaring

'U'
Mandukya Upanishad: dream state—play of principles
Fractal Ladder: V-state—Service, Adventure, Knowledge, Harmony drivers

'A'
Mandukya Upanishad: waking state—form of things
Fractal Ladder: P-state—physical, vital, mental, intuitional building-blocks

Source: Author

We applied the physical–vital–mental fractal to Progress to surface a deeper architecture of the Fractal Ladder. It was found that this deeper architecture paralleled the notion of AUM as described in the Mandukya Upanishad. This led to a conclusion that the deepest nature of Progress is none other than that supposedly ever-present seed of things, AUM. This then perhaps stands as the seed-fractal behind the Fractal Ladder.

The following chapters will look at an alternative bases for business and leadership, leveraging off some of the findings in this chapter, particularly the motive forces of Service, Adventure, Knowledge, and Harmony.

10

Remaking the Business World

INTRODUCTION

So far, we have suggested that our world is marked by a fractal reality. Within the vortex of fractal dynamics, there is a Fractal Ladder which is the signature of Progress. We have examined various rungs of creation on this ladder from the point of view of the fundamental building-blocks that determine the active dynamics of that rung, and the necessity of the completion of the sun-marked physical–vital–mental fractal, were progress to happen at the level of that rung. Following this fractal is the key to entry to the Fractal Ladder, which, by nature, allows and promotes dynamics of accelerated and sustainable progress. We have also examined fractal properties that exist on the Fractal Ladder, and have taken a deeper look at Progress itself, that remarkable dynamic, to gain insight into the secret names behind the construction and operation of the Fractal Ladder. These examinations along with the alternative model of reality that they suggest are showing us pathways to a more sustainable world that is within our grasp.

We know that the current intensity of problems we are experiencing at the global level, from climate change, to a general financial breakdown, to increasing resource shortages, to increasing prices of commodities, to destruction of biomes and species, amongst many other severe problems, is the result of living a primarily vitally centered life at many different levels. The effects of big business can no longer be ignored, and the choices we continue to support as a society must go through a radical change. In order to fully comprehend the nature of our problem, it is necessary to examine several distinct but related fractals. These include the consumerism fractal, the business fractal, the global economy fractal, and the global society fractal. We live in the vital sphere in each of these, and through dynamics of influence and feedback, there is the reinforcing of an unsustainable way of being that must be altered at the root.

In this chapter, we will look at each of the business-related fractals mentioned, and the resultant nature of the wake-up call. We will then seek to understand the serious global problems at its roots. We will conclude the chapter by considering possible approaches to then address the problems at its very roots by bringing about the needed shift from the vital to the mental way of being.

THE CONSUMERISM FRACTAL AND THE NATURE OF THE WAKE-UP CALL

As consumers, we have a choice of consuming dictated by the physical, vital, or mental way of being. In the physical way of being, there are certain set habits that determine our choices of consumption. Things we are used to doing, foods we are used to eating, clothes we are used to wearing, determine our on-going choices of consumption. We will not deviate from that much. In the vital way of being, there is far less stability in our choices, and stoked by desires, whims, and opportunities to experience immediate satisfaction we become conspicuous consumers. In this, the disposable type of product is promoted. There is little value for what it takes to create product and what the implications are of churning out more product on the environment and the segments of societies that create the inputs for the products or the products themselves. There is little or no thought or consideration given to the fact that equilibrium must be maintained with the earth of which we are a part. Reason rarely dawns at the height of the unrefined vital level. As long as base emotions—vanity, easing of jealousy, desire, amongst others—are fulfilled, that is all that counts. In the mental way of being, there is a dawning and even a more rigorous intervention of thought. In this case, consumerism will tend to become more sustainable in its essence, as larger impacts of buying decisions are progressively factored into the buying decision itself. This progression through the consumerism fractal is depicted in Figure 10.1.

Generally speaking, it is the immediate satisfaction of a desire, or a particular tendency that we may have created,

FIGURE 10.1   The Consumerism Fractal

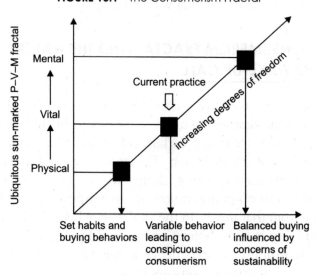

Progression of consumerism

Source: Author

or that may have incarnated in us as a result of affinity with that particular influence that drives our buying decisions. Even though at the leading edge there is the emergence of green consumers, that fact that the Wal-Marts of the world, with all their questionable impacts on social, cultural, and environmental dimensions are still growing so rapidly is a testament to the fact that we are, primarily speaking, at the vital level in the consumerism fractal. This positioning is also depicted in Figure 10.1.

It is not thought, but desire that drives much of our decision when it comes to buying. Yet, this is because those desires live in us, and obviously dominate our active consciousness. Unless this root dynamic is changed, the consumerism fractal will always remain at the vital level, and by nature of its reality and fractal influence, will cause other fractals at progressively more complex levels of organization, such as the business fractal, the global economy fractal, and the global society fractal to tend to remain locked at the vital level as well. As long as a questionable way of being is confined within boundaries, it may be allowed to exist in its sub-optimal way of being. When its influence effects the very foundation on which all boundaries depend, and if there is a meaning to that foundation, and we have seen that there is meaning in our lives as is evident by the existence of Progress, then there has to be a wake-up call that fundamentally attempts to re-align the way of being, and in this case, the many business-related fractals with the sun-marked physical–vital–mental fractal that is the very symbol of that Progress. This relationship is depicted in Figure 10.2.

Climate change is the very essence of that wake-up call. It causes the base dynamics and the long built-up equilibrium of our physical world to shift substantially. The increase of carbon dioxide and other greenhouse gases, due to man-made

FIGURE 10.2 The Necessity of a Wake-up Call

Arrestation of global system fractal at vital level requires global wake-up call

>> Climate change
>> Wake-up call X
>> Wake-up call Y

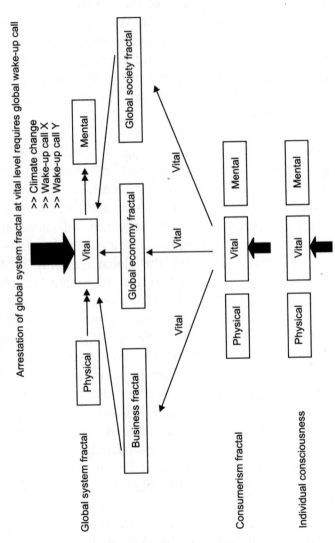

Source: Author

causes, increases the heat trapped in the atmosphere. As a result, temperatures shift upwards causing intense weather and storm systems around the world. Coastal towns and cities in the path of these storms get devastated.[1] Also, as polar ice melts, the water-level of seas and oceans increases, and again coastal regions, cities, and natural dams and wetlands get flooded and destroyed. As the oceans get warmer, fundamental water currents that have maintained the rhythm of seasons and weather of entire continents gets compromised and radical and destructive shifts to much larger ecosystems result. The increased atmospheric temperatures also results in alteration of ecosystems and long-established equilibrium of plants and animal species and contribute to their extinction. Diversity of life is compromised. The increased carbon dioxide levels also increases the acidity of the oceans, destroying the formation of base species, such as plankton at the very bottom of the marine food-chain, thereby also throwing all marine life into substantial disequilibrium and progressive extinction as well. As the fundamental equilibrium of oceans and lands and the many ecosystems that exist in these systems alters, base services that nature offers us, whether of carbon sequestration, purification of air and water, enrichment of soil, flood control, diversification of species with their many known and unknown benefits such as pollination, provision of medicinal compounds, creation of all types of food, amongst many other services that allow us to live as a human species, gets severely compromised and the very basis we depend on for all our lives gets pulled away from us.

As Figure 10.2 suggests, climate change has to be addressed by addressing the root-cause responsible for it. If this does not happen, then other wake-up calls—X and Y (indicated in upper right-hand corner of Figure 10.2) will arise in its place.

OTHER RELATED FRACTALS AND THEIR STATUS

In Chapter 3, we discussed the physical, vital, and mental outlooks of a business corporation. Our earlier analysis of business was focused more on looking at why the sun-marked physical–vital–mental fractal was the optimum path for business. But even as we look at where business is today, we must conclude that it too is at the vital level. The very fact that human life and humane working conditions requires a business case to be justified shows the short-sighted, self-seeking, and narrow focus that is characteristic of the vital level of operation. We would not expect otherwise, since the reason or prize of markets, the consumer, is himself at the vital level as just discussed.

The global economy fractal is also, as we discussed in Chapter 4, on the vital side of the boundary between the vital and the mental. This boundary, by nature, must bring up the essence of being vital in all its force, so that by understanding this and overcoming it, the very engine of the transition from the vital to the mental can come into being. Hence it is to be expected that all the depravities of this way of being must surface. Wars for oil, diamonds, and other metals, pillaging and ravishing entire countries and continents and sending millions into a sub-human state of life; shortages of fundamental resources such as water and clean air; shortages of staple foods as they become raw material for substitutes for oil; exploitation and destruction of biomes and long-formed and essential creations of earth, such as forest, wetlands, and watersheds; and trading of human beings as commodities to be sold into labor and satisfaction or pleasure, amongst other depravities promises to unleash further havoc on our already increasingly fragile way of life.

The global society fractal is in such a stage that all its institutions are currently judged by their ability to prop up and feed the engines of business. We seem to have forgotten knowledge for its own sake, but judge its value in its ability to create more money. We seem to have forgotten the promise of freedom contained in beautiful art and music, and have in a miserly deal, revalued these in terms of the money they can generate. Love is sold in the marketplace, and when a child is educated, it is often with the goal of churning out another asset that can at the end of the day benefit the bottom-line of business. Today, we talk of the triple bottom-line, and while this represents a progressive step away from the depravities of business, it is still the bottom-line and the institution of business that drives our meaning and our worth. At the end of the day, we have even forgotten that we can be something other than cogs or even fountains in the game of business. We have forgotten that there are other drivers of progress that if pursued along their own paths of development may result in a balance of creation necessary for truer sustainability. The sense of business has pervaded our lives so strongly that the meaning of societies and their very progress has become synonymous with the progress of business. This state of being indicates that the global society fractal too is in the vital phase. But again, why should we expect anything different, if in our basic stance as individuals we view life from a vital perspective.

THE ROOT OF THE PROBLEM

If all the rungs of our life are centered at the vital level, and if the meanings of our lives have become synonymous with business, we are in essence out of balance. The degree of this loss of balance is severe, as evident by the response from earth itself in the form of climate change. For in its essence, climate change is nothing other than a rebellion of matter. We are aware of rebellions through history, of a social nature, as means to bring development back into balance. But a rebellion of matter on the scale we are seeing today is perhaps unprecedented in recorded history. But why should there not be a rebellion of this nature, if indeed earth-system is a living being, with a trajectory of development that is in essence being compromised by the short-sighted way of her constructs? There is perhaps no other way for the trajectory of progress to continue as it should, unless individual consciousness, the root of the world fractal we see playing itself out now, were itself to progress to the next phase in its own sun-marked physical–vital–mental journey. That is the need of the hour. This change lies at the crux of the remaking of business to bring about true and meaningful sustainability.

There is no other way to promote true sustainability. Today, we see the rise of the Corporate Social Responsibility (CSR) movement.[2] In its essence, CSR is about integrating more holistic environmental, social, and governance consi-derations and factors into the strategy and operations of business. At its best, it is about pushing the business fractal from a vital to a more mental mode of operation. But at the end of the day, there is a real business case for adopting CSR, which means that business actors have a business incentive to follow through with what CSR brings to the table. The shift from vital to mental, from operating without more holistic environmental, social and governance considerations to operating with these considerations will allow a business to generate more profit. This is because more customers and stakeholders from the public to the investment community expect this behavior from business and therefore reward it. It is because it has also proven to minimize a variety of production and operating costs thereby increasing margins. Also because a consideration of environmental, social, and governance factors provides stimulus to the redefinition and creation of new products it enhances revenue generation. The point is that there is a business reason to make these changes; therefore, the mode of operation will tend to be centered in the unrefined profit motive which is essentially vital in nature. Because of the business case, business actors can hence remain fundamentally at the vital level, while doing all the things that CSR will make them do, to give the appearance that there has been a real shift to the mental level. But, no real shift has occurred, and the base fractal at the individual level remains at the vital level continuing to have its prolonging, and as we have seen, negative effect on world dynamics. At best, more mental force has been drawn to the service of the central vital principle.

The dangers of climate change may be immediately assuaged and we may live comforted that we have successfully addressed a potential calamity. But this is an illusion. The calamity has only been pushed back into the future. The fundamental way of being remains vital, and therefore this dynamic is what will continue to ripple outward to the limit of the earth, just as in the case of climate change, which has rippled out to the limits of the earth.

We know, for instance, that the increase in electronic goods introduces a distortion to the natural electromagnetic field that surrounds each living being. We are essentially electromagnetic entities and this continued vital hunger for electronics of all kinds, in every facet of our lives, will continue to compromise the basic dynamics of our individual chemical equilibriums. For all chemistry that occurs in us is a result of a subtle electromagnetic equilibrium that stimulates cellular level chemical reactions.[3] With the increase of electronics and even with their increasingly being implanted into our very bodies, whether through devices such as attachable cell phones and receptors or probes that enter into the bloodstream, the possibility that we are setting ourselves up for a severe disequilibrium as catastrophic as climate change cannot be ignored.

But there are so many other micro-threats of this nature that compromise our very equilibrium as individual entities. There is also the infiltration of harmful chemicals that alter our body chemistry, whether through intake of industrialized and processed foods and pharmaceuticals, application of cosmetics that immediately enter into our bloodstreams, use of cleaners, washers, paints, and other similar materials that exist in our dwellings, regular contact with surfaces such as processed textiles, plastics, automobiles and other forms of transport that are themselves centers for the release of myriad harmful chemicals, and ingestion of non-renewable energy sources such as oil and gas that again pervade every aspect of the society and life we have today created for ourselves. There are a thousand ways that we are oblivious of whereby compromising chemicals can enter into our bodily systems. And there are a thousand ways in which they enter into the very fiber of nature, right from wastes released during manufacturing, leakages during transportation, off-gassing during storage, not to mention as wastes released from us through course of daily activity. Industries that we have created—consumer products, energy, food and agriculture, transportation, information technology and electronics— have, through our vital lust, become means to kill our very vitality.[4]

Climate change is in fact a wake-up call to this vital way of being, and so long as we are able to penetrate into the true cause of it, and grapple with the root fractal of which it is the result (see Figure 10.2), climate change will have done a great service to humankind by causing the required shift in our way of being from a vital to a more mental way of being. The root pattern at the individual level is what must be changed. If however, we reduce greenhouse gas emissions, create clever trading schemes and markets for promoting services of nature, force regulation and legislation that causes business to alter action without affecting the root cause, we will have done ourselves little favor, and will be pushing back the inevitable catastrophe, which may incarnate in another form, whether of a fundamental poisoning of life through chemical overdose, or a destabilization of living matter through alteration of base electromagnetics, or some other way that we are not foreseeing.

FACILITATING THE SHIFT FROM THE VITAL TO THE MENTAL

The shift from the vital to the mental level at the individual level is an imperative. The transition must be made, either willingly through sincere individual, corporate, and societal effort, or unwillingly through potential catastrophes of the nature of climate change. The movement from a vital to a mental way of being is at the crux of the matter, and the question is what can business do, or how must it be remade in order to promote that shift? Several potential approaches have suggested themselves through the course of the book.

One is to have people consciously examine the tendencies that exist within them, and through reason and thought, invigorate the arrested journey that has caused the tendency to anchor around its state of particular dysfunction. This is no doubt a difficult approach that few may be inclined to follow. Another approach that has suggested itself is to consciously enter into relationship with Progress and lay everything before it. If this can be done it is probably the best approach and we will have more to say about this in the next chapter. Given the fact that the business world is primarily at the vital level, however, and that this type of thought may be too much of a leap for it, this too may be a difficult path to follow. A third approach is to mobilize the secret names of Progress. We had posited a fourth phase, that of intuition, that lay beyond the mental phase. This phase is alive with a dynamic array of motive forces, the secret names, that we found are also responsible for the very creation of the Fractal Ladder that cuts across creation. These motive forces are service, adventure, knowledge, and harmony.

These motive forces are at the heart of Progress, and given that we are all constructs of Progress, it must be that these motive forces lie at the heart of what drives us, too. The physical, vital, and mental states are settled though unrefined formations of service, adventure, and knowledge, respectively. Harmony stands behind it and emerges more as we move into the fourth or the intuitional state. Hence, service, adventure, knowledge, and harmony, are embedded in each living entity. In the vast play of nature, differentiation seems to manifest as unique combinations of these four motive forces. Countries, communities, mature companies, people, each seem to have different combinations of these four forces that determine their uniqueness. Each living being, hence, likely has one of these four forces as a dominant driver of their being, with the other motive forces settled around or supporting the prime driver in different ways. This is depicted in Figure 10.3.

For illustrative purposes, Figure 10.3 depicts Entity-1 ruled by a dominant "Adventure/Power" component and Entity-2 as being ruled by a dominant "Service/Perfection" component. Entities could be people, companies, collectivities, or countries, amongst other mature organizations.

In the new creation of business, it is these fundamental drivers, hence, that must be mobilized as the bases of the foundation. In today's world, we are mobilized as pieces in the global business puzzle. The possibility of what we stand for is reduced to one questionable motive force—that

FIGURE 10.3   The Play of Uniqueness

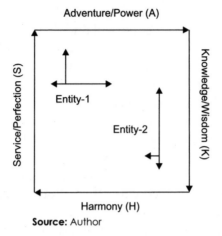

Source: Author

of exploitation in the name of business. In the remaking of business this reality has to be changed. The four motive forces that must stand at the base of any vibrant creation have to be consciously brought forward. Even though their fuller action may belong to the fourth or intuitional state, a conscious over-reaching of the mental way of being to mobilize these four powers cannot but result in a more fruitful journey into and through the mental phase. This has to be the case if these four powers stand as the basis of uniqueness, and as we have posited, the very essence of the mental way of being is to question and, therefore, to anyway more rapidly arrive at this very sense of uniqueness, which is embodied by various combinations of the four motive forces at the heart of Progress as illustrated in Figure 10.3.

Business to-date has proceeded along the vital dimension which is the shadow-state of adventure. In this shadow-state, the prime motive force has often been that of exploitation at any cost. This is, for obvious and already observed reasons, a miserly and unsustainable basis for organizational foundation. This very foundation has to be changed to include the four dimensions of service, adventure, knowledge, and harmony. It is only so that the true and sustainable springs or progress will be mobilized; that people will find that their raison d'être coincides with the activity of business; and that the very nature of Progress can incarnate in the activity of business thereby changing its fibers for ever. The incarnation takes place through the root component—people. People who are allowed to follow their essential and innate way of being create the reality of progress at the individual level, and then by fractal pressure, at each subsequent level.

Climate change and other threats of a similar nature can only be securely changed when the pattern at the root of the global fractal is allowed to move to the next phase in its own journey through mobilization of the deep forces that stand at the heart of Progress. Even a brief study of sustainable society, countries, or other complex organizations through history will reveal that those with enduring power have managed to mobilize something of the four motive forces simultaneously. Severe instability is caused when only one motive force, which by definition lacks influence from the other motive forces and is unable to move out of its unrefined state, remains the basis of organization.[5] Witness the current degeneration of countries as different as the USA on the one hand and Pakistan on the other, that seem have been locked into an adamant and single way of being, thereby destroying their very springs of progress. As mentioned, in the business world today everyone is subsumed to exist for the unrefined vital urge of exploitation. This may take other, more pleasant names, but at the end of the day, if a business does not fulfill its financial goals, all manner of idealism is often jettisoned. This standardization at the people level to force thoughts and acts to be of a certain kind only is the great tragedy of current corporate life.

The question as to whether the institution of business can remake itself to allow a balanced play of the four motive forces simultaneously, lies at the heart of its sustainability. On the one hand, it can be envisioned that current business organizations may rise to the challenge and truly allow the four ways of being to incarnate at the very foundation of their operations. On the other hand, it can be envisioned that the poison runs just too deep, and that this type of model will need to be newly incubated into being. In the second scenario perhaps it is at the grassroots community level that the new models will come into being. After all, some of the perversities of modern business are attributed to its separation from ground realities and from accountability to society in general. A grassroots community-level organization will perhaps be more likely to reinforce these checks to thereby minimize the vital exaggerations that more naturally accompany a context of minimal accountability. It also has the added advantage of more naturally nurturing the four motive forces in close albeit perhaps independent proximity to each other. The proximity may allow for more intimate interaction from the start thereby evolving more robust organizations over time.

Though a particular form of the organization may tend to allow the more balanced play of motive forces, it cannot be the deciding factor. The deciding factor is the kind of leadership that exists at the individual level. The individual leader is going to determine the degree to which the heart of Progress can be mobilized. The individual leader is going to determine the degree to which uniqueness and the countering of established ways of being can come into being.

SUMMARY

In this chapter, we studied several fractals related to business to understand the nature of the problem we face on a global scale. The degree of the problem is apparent in the nature of the wake-up call—climate change. We argued that climate change is only a symptom and unless addressed at its very roots, by shifting the seed-fractal at the base of the related business fractals, we are doing ourselves little long-term favor. We discussed the nature of the root and suggested approaches to remaking the business world thereby allowing a fruitful transition from the vital to the mental way of being. We suggested that mobilization of motive forces and effective leadership were the keys to facilitating the needed shift. In the next chapter, we will examine the criticality and nature of the required leadership.

11

Future Leadership

INTRODUCTION

We live in a world predominantly animated by the physical and the vital, to some extent the mental, and less so by the intuitional way of being. Examination of several rungs of creation reveals that it is these very states that form the building-blocks of these levels of creation. So long as the preponderant state at a level remains the physical or vital or even the lower mental way of being, as opposed to the side of the mental approaching the intuitional, conditions at that level of creation will tend to be more as a thing of the past as opposed to progressively focused. This means that our thoughts, behaviors, and actions will reinforce a surface rendering of ourselves, and we will continue as cogs in a machinery set in motion through past laws. We will continue an existence as puppets of dominant physically-centered, backward-pointing forces.

The prime task of leadership, hence, regardless of the field, is to bring about this shift from a physical–vital to a mental–intuitional mode of operation. That is, an organization's sun-marked physical–vital–mental fractal, regardless of type of organization and respective playing-field, must be completed.

In this chapter, we will look at types of leadership and focus on a particular kind of leadership—holistic leadership—which is the need of the hour, and on its development. We will then focus on the development of the deeper drivers, or of a leader's *dharma*, which is a particularly potent way of developing holistic leadership. We will conclude this chapter with an examination of the repertoire of tools, techniques, and approaches available to the Fractal Ladder leader.

TYPES OF LEADERSHIP

If Progress is a reality, and the examinations in this book conclude that this must be so, there have to be circumstances in the affairs of life that perforce move in a direction consistent with the sun-marked physical–vital–mental fractal in spite of any number of forces to the contrary. This is how progress happens. For this to occur, the particular circumstance must be the field of an instrument by which the necessary shifts occur along the needed trajectory. If it is an unknowing instrument, that is, one who is not aware of the intention and hand of Progress in the movement of circumstance, yet he or she likely must have mastery over some critical elements—be it physical, vital or mental—the application of which allows the circumstance to move in the needed direction.

Physical mastery may take the form of a precise knowledge of the rules and the resources that have established past stability, and therefore of insight into the right application of these variables to ensure that stability continues or incrementally changes in the needed manner. Vital mastery may take the form of power to be able to shift players who make the rules, through insight into what their emotional or resource levers of change are. Mental mastery may take the form of insight into root causes of stability and shifts in the situation and the adjustment of these to bring about sizable changes in circumstance. In the case of the unknowing instrument, it is still the intent of Progress that likely acts in a subtle manner to cause the unknowing instrument to choose in a particular way so that overall progress in the circumstance occurs.

The mastery over the physical, vital, or mental elements of the situation are, no doubt, themselves manifestations of leadership. This kind of "element" leadership, however, is different from the integral, holistic leadership that is the need of the hour in that it is in a manner of speaking disconnected from Progress and therefore incomplete. Were it to be consciously connected to the very fount of Progress, it would admit to a whole other way of operation because it would by definition be open to the mysteries and possibilities inherent in Progress and through this influence would likely be stretched beyond anything it could possibly effectuate in the absence of that influence. The contrast in type of leadership is summarized in Figure 11.1.

Connection and mobilization of Progress will allow the substance from the heart of Progress to project more of it forward, and truer, more spontaneous, creative and sustainable and enduring renderings of service and perfection, adventure, knowledge, and harmony will manifest. In other words, truer, and more unique personalities of deeper substance, radically different from the established personalities and commonly accepted stereotypes of leaders of the past will be experienced. This is not to say that these types of personalities have not manifested in the past; they surely have. Conscious contact with Progress, however, will likely cause more of these types of leaders to manifest.

It is this type of leadership that is the need of the hour. This is so, because it is nothing less than an "omniscience" or "omnipotence" or "omnicaring" or "omnipresence" of the type

FIGURE 11.1   Contrast in Leadership Type

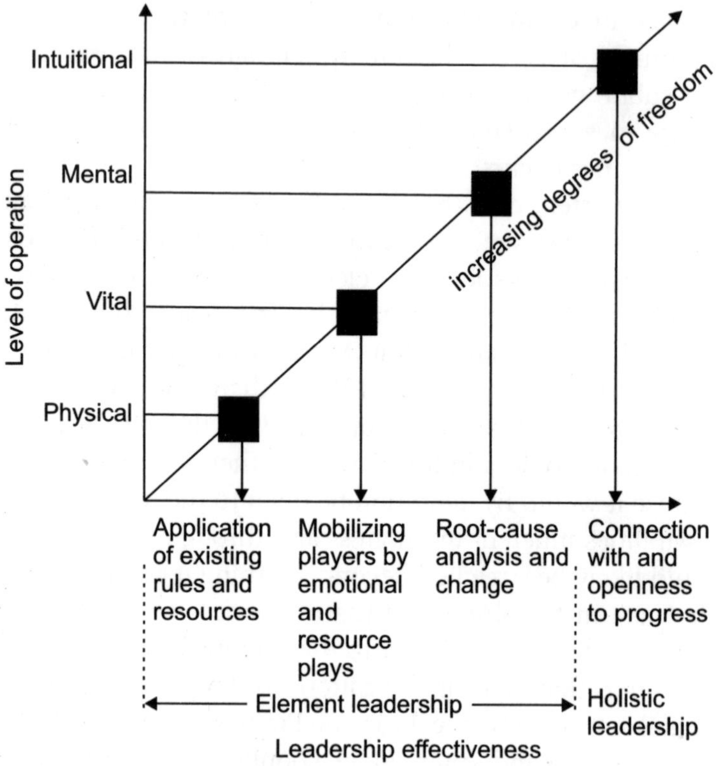

Source: Author

possessed by Progress that is perhaps needed to successfully handle the many different complexities humanity is currently embroiled in. It is also the need of the hour that true personalities with power to counter established tendencies and habits arise. If a personality is composed of the same dynamics and habits already present in established physical, vital, and mental building-blocks, then by definition, this is likely only going to reinforce past rule. It is only by new and un-established dynamics manifesting and restructuring existing building-blocks that past habits have a chance of being countered. Such personalities can only incarnate by being in more conscious relation with Progress. This is the only sure way for a habitual difference that becomes permanent to be created. Anchoring newer possibility to anything that is the result of the past, even a mental idea, is potentially too replete with contradictions, subtle or overt, to be the basis of a new creation.

This highest possibility of leadership can only take place when the instrument or leader has disengaged from the physical, vital, and mental trappings, so that it is not their dynamics that move it, but the deeper intent resonant with Progress that in fact guides the physical, vital, and mental instrumentation toward the needed outcome. The highest possibility of leadership can only take place when a new personality summarizing new possibility emerges in the play of life. When this occurs, the leader truly becomes a dynamic being because the inner integrates with the outer thereby also creating the conditions for maximum affectivity.

To connect inner power to global change means that it is not physical power, not vital power, not even mental power that must be the fount of our existence, though each of these will, and even must be, used in our expression of leadership. It is the deeper essence of our realities, that essence which finds its meaning and motive in Progress itself, and inner power that must become the fount of our being. It is Progress that must incarnate in us. Only so will we become centers of creative power.

DEVELOPMENT OF HOLISTIC LEADERSHIP

The means by which this different way of operating, moving from a stasis of physical or vital or mental power to a deeper basis of power, can manifest are numerous. For the opportunity to exercise deeper power exists at every stretch, turn and moment of our lives. This must be since we simultaneously participate at several levels of creation where the present-day dynamic is an expression of a stalled sun-marked physical–vital–mental journey. The more we are able to recognize the stagnation and cause these journeys to continue on their inevitable paths of progress, the more does Progress itself incarnate in us, and the more do we assume that mantle of leadership that is the meaning and drives towards effective completion of our lives.

In the face of opposition, the more we truly stand up for ourselves, the more will the truth of what we are manifest. Leadership is about manifesting the truth of who we are. It is about bringing out into relief the aspects of Progress that current-day life tends to subdue. It is also about causing movement of the various stagnated fractals that animate our lives so that the general and prevalent vital arrestation can be reversed and each fractal can complete its sun-marked physical–vital–mental journey. Finally, it is about stepping on the Fractal Ladder to more proactively and consciously align with Progress.

The imperative for leadership of this nature is unquestionable. As already discussed, we are faced with problems in every arena of life from the most external to the most internal. Matter itself, our very basis of life, is rebelling against us in the form of global movements such as climate change. Our very definition of ourselves has sunk to a level of poverty where our worth is equated to the acquisition of money or in our ability to participate in the global business machinery. The need to reorient ourselves so that we align with the heart of meaning and creation is a necessity. We need a redefinition on every level of creation starting from who we are to what our world is. This is the task and necessity of leadership in the 21st century. In fully embracing this task, holistic leadership will, of necessity, begin to surface more and more, because the task itself is deeply aligned with pushing the ubiquitous sun-marked physical–vital–mental fractal to its next phase in many independent journeys.

But there will likely be a gradient by which this leadership manifests in us. This gradient can be revealed by an application of the physical, vital, mental fractal architecture to the notion of holistic leadership itself. The seed-idea is captured in Figure 11.2.

FIGURE 11.2   Development of Holistic Leadership

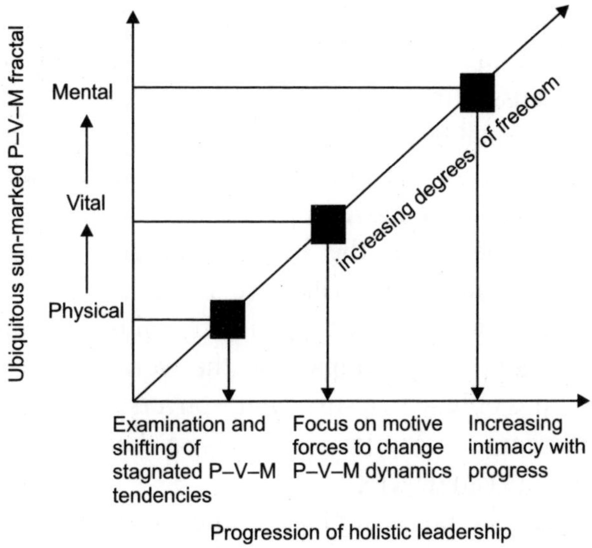

Source: Author

Figure 11.2 brings together several approaches to development of holistic leadership that have surfaced through the course of the book, in a sequence that makes more sense from a developmental point of view. As a first stage, representative of the physical level, stagnated physical, vital, and mental tendencies can be examined to bring about corresponding shifts in arrestation. We had discussed this in Chapter 2—The Person Pattern. Examination of the current way our physical, vital, and mental building-blocks function must in fact be a pre-requisite to their changing. In fact, a number of fractal properties we had discussed in Chapter 8, and in particular the physical, the vital, and the mental properties (see Figure 8.1) that have to do with the structure of the Fractal Ladder can also be leveraged to bring about shifts in arrestation.

At the vital level, deeper motive forces, service, adventure, knowledge, harmony, are invoked by putting these into practice in our lives. These will have a direct effect on changing our physical, vital, and mental building-blocks and will be discussed in more detail later.

At the mental level, the instrument, having gone through the preparation of the physical and vital stages, will now be more ready to be moved by the suggestions, in-rushing, and possibilities from the heart of Progress. Surrender, conversation, alignment will have more meaning once a different and more unique type of personality that can have a different and unique impact on the world has begun to manifest. It is only so that surrender, conversation, alignment can really come to fruition. It is only so that true intimacy with Progress can develop.

Whereas the physical phase of the development can be tedious, without it, it may be difficult for one to even admit of the need of a new way of operating. The vital phase, that of invoking the deeper drivers or motive forces, is however of a completely different nature. It is more dynamic and living and will cause people to change willingly because of the inevitability of the approach and because it addresses the deeper need of who each one is seeking to and who each one must become—in other words, what each person's *dharma* is.

DEVELOPMENT OF *DHARMA*

As Progress incarnates within us, we realize that its nature is our nature and that who we are and who we must become is determined by what Progress is and what it is perhaps, in its manifested aspect, seeking to become. In Chapter 9, on the nature of Progress, we had suggested that it too could be thought of as having a physical, vital, and mental component (see Figure 9.5). In its physical or most tangible aspect, it appears to us as the very building-blocks of all levels of creation—the physical, the vital, the mental, and the intuitional ways of being. In its vital or dynamic aspect, it appears to us as pragmatic motive forces of service, adventure, knowledge, and harmony. In its mental aspect, it appears to us as omnipresence, omnipotence, omniscience, and omnicaring.

In other words, while we are presently physical–vital–mental and partly intuitional beings, and tend to live our lives determined by which part of the being is more in front or more active so that we may be predominantly physical, or predominantly vital, or predominantly mental in outlook and nature, yet who we are tending to become is in itself revealed by examination of the "vital" and "mental" aspects of Progress. This is inevitable given that like any other sun-marked physical–vital–mental fractal, the physical aspect of Progress must yield to its vital and subsequently to its mental aspect. Hence, through the motive forces of service, adventure, knowledge, and harmony, the "vital" aspects of Progress, we begin to alter the very physical or tangible aspect of Progress within ourselves so that the journey of the physical aspect of Progress does not only get completed to tend towards the intuitional way of being (see Action 1 in Figure 11.3), therefore even more securely surfacing our uniqueness or dharma, but each of the states of the physical

FIGURE 11.3 Double-action of Motive Forces

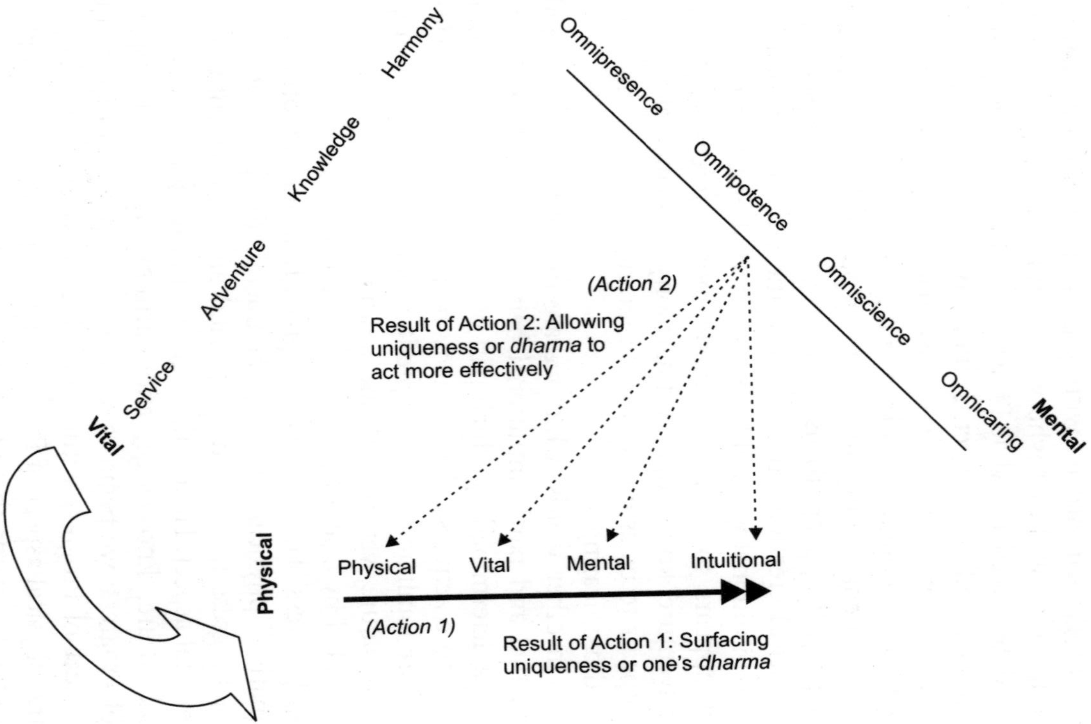

Omnipresence   Omnipotence   Omniscience   Omnicaring

Mental

Harmony
Knowledge
Adventure
Service

Vital

Physical

Physical   Vital   Mental   Intuitional

(Action 2)

Result of Action 2: Allowing uniqueness or *dharma* to act more effectively

(Action 1)

Result of Action 1: Surfacing uniqueness or one's *dharma*

Source: Author

aspect themselves are also altered to admit of more of the "mental" aspect of Progress as described by the terms omnipresence, omnipotence, omniscience, and omnicaring (see Action 2 in Figure 11.3), thereby allowing our dharma through more capable physical, vital, and mental building-blocks to express itself more completely. This is depicted in Figure 11.3.

Put in another way, through the adoption of our more dynamic nature or *dharma*, of service or adventure or knowledge or harmony, or even the reorientation of our lives to experiment with the meaning and expression of each of these possibilities together or in sequence, as opposed to the meager and bankrupt demand of life as business that we find ourselves embedded in today, the nature of each part of our being—the physical, the vital, the mental—get expanded to embrace more of the essential qualities of Progress defined by omnipresence, omnipotence, omniscience, and omnicaring, and the fourth or intuitional part of the being, that which expresses more of our inner uniqueness and identity—our *dharma*—begins more securely to come to the surface.

It is the increasing surety of one's own *dharma* coming to the surface that causes stagnations in individual fractal journeys to be overcome. For it is then that the obstinacies and rigidities of the physical, the aggressions and self-seeking of the vital, and the limited ideas and narrow reasoning of the mental, can yield to a more complete basis of being.

Imagine, for instance, if the spirit of service and perfection is invoked. Perhaps, it is the accompanying urge to do things perfectly, or to delve into the details, or to surrender to the task at hand in such a manner, that the heart of Progress itself comes alive in these movements. In such a situation, if the person who has awakened this deep urge has tended to be anchored in the physical outlook, this urge is perhaps the most foolproof way of guiding him into the vital, and even the mental outlook, so that the encasing or contextual fractal is able to complete its fractal journey. The same is true if the spirit of adventure or the spirit of knowledge or the spirit of harmony is invoked. These drivers have their own power and can have the effect of breaking held limits when a person abandons themselves to them. The more one completes one's respective fractal journeys, the more does any stagnation disappear; thus, one's uniqueness or *dharma* comes more to the surface. This then puts a virtuous cycle into existence. In the virtuous cycle, the removal of stagnations allows the very substance of the physical, the vital, and the mental to change, which thereby further open to the action of the other drivers. Incarnating something of these drivers is also the surest way of assuring sustainable and progressive movement since the physical, the vital, and the mental are themselves only diminished representations of the potential inherent in each of the deeper drivers.

As already discussed in Chapter 9, in the heart of progress, these drivers act simultaneously. When this type of action, the simultaneity of service and adventure and knowledge and harmony, can happen in the physical, vital, and mental, the balance of development will have been tipped away from its orientation toward the inertia of yesteryear, and a more progressive and rapid development will likely manifest. For, more of Progress will be pouring itself into the inertias and stagnations and biases and narrowness to thereby more assuredly move them out of these habitual responses. Service without adventure, knowledge, and harmony will tend to create the inertias of the physical. Adventure without service, knowledge, and harmony will tend to create the aggressions and self-seeking the vital. Knowledge without service, adventure, and harmony will tend to create the narrowness and impotencies of the mental. Hence, the more each of these four deeper drivers can manifest in each of the fundamental building-blocks, the more assuredly will the nature and possibilities represented by the fundamental building-blocks begin to change.

Personality too, now hinged around a more securely surfacing *dharma*, will begin to go through a fundamental shift. From a bases of established and often destructive or narrow patterns that do nothing more than reinforce the already established dynamics of yesteryear, personality will flourish in new directions representative of service and perfection, of adventure and courage, of knowledge and seeking, of harmony and mutuality. These will introduce new and different dynamics into the established order of things, and new possibilities will consequently begin to appear.

Incarnating leaders means that it is these drivers that need to incarnate. Imagine a world where the spirit of service and perfection, the spirit of adventure, the spirit of knowledge, and the spirit of harmony are organically alive in every field of life. Imagine a world where these drivers, occultly tasked with progressing the destiny of humankind, for this has to be the case if Progress is a reality and if these drivers emanate from the heart of Progress, are freely allowed to interact with each other and enrich each other without encumbrance caused by such concerns as short-term financial returns. Endeavors proceed because of the love of service, or because there is pure knowledge to be gained, or because there is adventure and new discovery to be had, or because there is a new level of harmony to be established. Caution and calculation, monetary returns from investments, narrow self-seeking and fulfillment of desire, proving of one's own point of view at the expense of any truth contained in another's point of view, and other similar yesteryear heuristics that animate much of our practical life today are cast aside. A new modus operandi that mirrors the deep essence of Progress comes into being instead.

REPERTOIRE OF THE FRACTAL LADDER LEADER

There are a range of approaches that are available to the Fractal Ladder leader to address the dynamics of different types of organizations at different levels. These are summarized in Figure 11.4.

The Fractal Ladder leader has to operate from a mental–intuitional orientation. The physical, vital, and mental properties on the left side of Figure 11.4 summarize Fractal Ladder system characteristics. These are the means by which common-place dynamics and definitions need to be reinterpreted. The definitions of organizations, the active dynamics that animate them, the reasons why organizations exist, the best way in which they can be developed, the alignment of purpose with contextual systems, the addressing of obstacles that may arise in their functioning needs to emanate from an understanding of these Fractal Ladder properties, and needs to leverage them in solving any problem. Our current approach to the organizational situations we encounter are based on an inaccurate rendering of isolationist or physical–vital based reality. The reinterpretation of our operating systems in terms of the fractal-animated systems-based Fractal Ladder brings us closer to a more accurate rendering of reality, and will therefore greatly assist the leader in his or her approach to arriving at solutions.

This system is a manifestation of a ubiquitous sun-marked physical–vital–mental fractal. It is therefore in constant progression. Our analysis, especially in Chapter 9, reveals how the system is likely to evolve, with the increasing manifestation of the deeper drivers that represent individual dharma. This is, in fact, system inevitability. These drivers, as we have discussed earlier in this chapter, have to become active even to counter arrestation of the many instances of

FIGURE 11.4 The Repertoire of the Fractal Ladder Leader

Understanding and Shifting the Fractal Ladder			Relationship with Progress	
Physical	**Vital**	**Mental**	**Invoking drivers**	**Developing intimacy**
Universality	Intersection	World-wiseliness	Service and Perfection	Alignment
Influence	Flow	Mirroring	Adventure and Power	Aspiration
Recursion	Facilitation	Affirmation	Knowledge and Wisdom	Surrender
Completion	Upscaling	Integration	Harmony	Rejection
Evolution		Uniqueness		Love
Matrixing				
Step-wise development				
Feedback				

Source: Author

the ubiquitous sun-marked physical–vital–mental fractal. In designing any kind of system, the play of these *dharmas* has to be centrally considered. The leader needs to successfully mobilize these drivers in the design and functioning of any manner of organization, be it at the person, corporation, or societal levels.

Finally, the notion of operating in a conscious, intelligent, purposeful, fully integrated system means that the design and sense of Progress needs to be more consciously invoked at every point in development. This can be done by developing intimacy with Progress, and hopefully becoming an even more conscious instrument in the unveiling of Progress' own designs. Without this, we are journeying on a rudderless ship. In a world animated by a number of fractal journeys, finer understanding of how circumstances can be interpreted in these terms, whether, for example, as the result of the intersection of independent fractal journeys, or as the attempt of upscaling, amongst other possibilities, will require intuition in the sense of clear guidance from Progress itself. Hence, the category of approaches, as reflected by the column on the right side of Figure 11.4 have also to be seriously developed and used by a Fractal Ladder leader.

SUMMARY

We began this chapter with a discussion of types of leadership. While recognizing the importance of element leadership, we concluded that holistic leadership is the need of the hour, especially given the surfacing reality of the Fractal Ladder system that we live in. We then focused on approaches to developing such holistic leadership, applying fractal architecture to the notion of holistic leadership to arrive at a reasonable progression for holistic leadership. While we definitely need to get to intimacy with Progress as a basis for holistic leadership, the necessity of being useful instruments in the scheme of things by being unique, *dharma*-based entities surfaced. This implies the emergence in oneself of some deep motive force represented by service and perfection or adventure and power or knowledge and wisdom or harmony, which in itself implies the remaking of the basic physical, vital, and mental building-blocks that constitute much of our personality, beginning first with examination of stagnation in these building-blocks. The lynch-pin of development, however, is the development of *dharma* and we looked at some of the dynamics related to that. We finally considered the whole repertoire of approaches available to the Fractal Ladder leader. It is this repertoire that must be utilized to address the plethora of compromising issues we currently exist in.

12

Alternative Futures

INTRODUCTION

The existence of Progress is a sure indication of the overall direction of development for humanity. The architecture of Progress, as indicated by its three aspects—physical, vital, mental—further indicates the trajectory of this development, since in one way of looking at the architecture the physical is about established reality, the vital is about reality in process of being created, and the mental is about possible reality. In its present "physical" incarnation the Fractal Ladder is animated by relatively unrefined physical, vital, and mental building-blocks. As the intuitional element surfaces, and as humans follow their inspiration, deeper drivers, or *dharmas*, service and perfection, adventure and courage, knowledge and wisdom, and harmony and mutuality will more surely come to the surface. The very structure and possibility of the fundamental building-blocks will alter and the physical will morph more into a physical–service–perfection conglomerate, the vital into a vital–adventure–courage conglomerate, the mental into a mental–knowledge–wisdom conglomerate and the intuitional will be more firmly established as an intuitional–harmony–mutuality conglomerate.

This will alter the base-fractal of which the Fractal Ladder is a creation, and hence each of its rungs will themselves become projections of the radically refined building-blocks. Much of experienced creation, from the individual to corporations to countries to society to the environment to planet earth, will begin to function in a more enlightened and obviously sustainably progressive way far more aligned with the deeper drivers of Progress. This can be thought of as the vital incarnation of the Fractal Ladder. But that is only a step along the way.

Even further in the future one can foresee the deeper "mental" aspect of Progress—of which omnipresence, omnipotence, omniscience, omnicaring are qualities—further altering the manifested character of the fundamental building-blocks so that the physical further morphs into a physical–service–perfection–omnipresence conglomerate, the vital morphs into a vital–adventure–courage–omnipotence conglomerate, the mental further morphs into a mental–knowledge–wisdom–omniscience conglomerate, and the intuitional further morphs into an intuitional–harmony–mutuality–omnicaring conglomerate. This can be thought of as the mental incarnation of the Fractal Ladder. The Fractal Ladder further alters and all possibility and apotheosis is then perhaps more obviously present at each and every moment of space and time. This is no doubt an astounding future.

The timing of these futures, of the manifestations of the discussed incarnations of the Fractal Ladder is, however, the issue in question. Depending on choices we make now and in the foreseeable future the promising incarnations of the Fractal Ladder will occur sooner or later. The interim passage is variable and expresses alternative paths, which because of the possibility of taking decades or even perhaps centuries will for all practical purposes need to be thought of in terms of alternative futures. The existence of Progress and its signature across creation, in the form of the Fractal Ladder, indicates that the promising incarnations are inevitable. Whether we arrive there through a path of major upheaval and destruction or through one of relative ease and joy, a sunlit path, depends on the degree to which we are able to complete the myriad sun-marked physical–vital–mental fractal journeys that each of us is continually on. The root, of course, of all the myriad journeys we all have the privilege of being on, which fractal mirroring, fractal influence, fractal evolution, fractal completion, fractal matrixing, amongst the other fractal properties points to, is the state of consciousness—physical, or vital, or mental, or intuitional—that we tend to operate from. The alternative futures that we will experience over the next few decades and even perhaps centuries is an outcome of the general state of consciousness that as a race we choose to be in.

In this chapter, we will look at various futures or scenarios that may arise depending to what extent a particular orientation becomes generalized in the mind of the public. These include the physical scenario, the vital scenario, the lower mental scenario, the higher mental scenario, and the intuitional scenario.

BASIS OF THE INTUITIONAL SCENARIO

At its crux the Fractal Ladder indicates a reality of deep connection and integration. Everything is inter-connected and everything is integrated around a reality of progress. Progress itself is the secret of the one system, and the Fractal Ladder represents the character of that Progress. The Fractal Ladder is the key to the system. Stepping on it unveils a world of sustainable and un-endable progress. It indicates a conscious, meaningful reality in which there are no accidents but all is the result of particular base patterns representative of the sun-marked physical–vital–mental pattern in the consciousness of its primary actors. These base patterns themselves get their reality from the possibility inherent in Progress and through force of creativity manifest as different actors represented by different types of organization on each rung of the ladder. It is possible too, and at present far more likely, that the physical, vital, mental building-blocks arrange themselves in other ways unaligned with the sun-marked pattern, in which case the organizations of which they are the constituents falls outside of the Fractal Ladder, in the region of the system characterized by a general fractal vortex. These organizations, too, can step on the Fractal Ladder if they are able to complete the fractal journey that characterizes their current reality. Completion of the fractal journey implies that uniqueness and true personality are beginning to manifest. For it is only so that the generally accepted realities of the past, that run counter to progress, can be overcome and the price for entry on the Fractal Ladder, as it were, paid as a result of that. Truer personality is aligned with the deeper drivers of Progress and begins through its action to even more rapidly change the very nature of the building-blocks and the Fractal Ladder.

Realization of the reality of this system means that the actor, whether individual, corporation, collectivity, or country, is operating at the intuitional level. Already, a comprehensiveness of vision and inspiration is animating the general outlook of the actor, and possibility, meaning, action are driven by a reality very different from that driven by the other building-blocks of possibility. This outlook will result in a shorter, more joyful, and easier path towards the future, and inevitable incarnations of the Fractal Ladder. On this path, each type of actor more quickly embraces the uniqueness they are capable of. Hence, people more quickly attune to their raison d'être, and casting aside the false promises of making the quick buck by becoming a part of the global business engine, follow the possibilities of service, or adventure, or knowledge, or harmony, as their *dharma* or character dictates.

A new array of fractals arises, and all manner of changes at each more complex level of organization—corporation, community, collectivity, country, society—comes into being. We will revisit the intuitional scenario later.

THE PHYSICAL SCENARIO

At the other end of the spectrum, a physical orientation by an actor would imply a reality dictated primarily by what the eye can see. The notion of a single-integrated system characterized by a Fractal Ladder would be an outright chimera or even blasphemy to the established way of seeing. The established way of seeing will be the unerring anchor-point and the filter through which all decisions should be made. Climate change, slow global poisoning, destabilization of all forms of magneto-chemical systems, destruction of environments and the resource base, are likely to be consigned to the category of hogwash and definitely not perceived as signs of rebellion from a conscious and progress-driven system. At most, these will be thought of as natural occurrences in a cycle that has existed from time immemorial. People and society will continue to be thought of as existing to lubricate the unerring business engine that has proven its value just the way it is time and time again. There will be no time nor need for searching for another way of being, because the one in existence now will be perceived as being perfect and in no want of change.

In this scenario, major catastrophe and upheaval is likely to happen suddenly. Obviously people will be utterly unprepared for what hits them. This scenario will be like that of the frog in slowly heating water. As the temperature of the water increases, rather than jumping out, the frog gets more used to it and does not even realize that something is amiss until it is too late and the water has started to boil. At this point it is not possible for the frog to escape and it too boils with the water. In this scenario systemic weakness is not addressed but simply covered up. This is the scenario of financial bailouts and stark denial. Leading countries maintain global economic power by the application of military might. Currencies are artificially propped up to maintain the semblance of strength. Religious institutions intervene to promote leaders from the past. The "American Dream" and way of life continue to be propagated as the best and strongest until it is too late. All the while, what really needs to be changed remains unaddressed.

THE VITAL SCENARIO

In the scenario marked by vital orientation the frenzies of today continue until exhaustion. This means that the pace of systemic debilitation will proceed faster than in the scenario marked by physical orientation. In the physical orientation scenario, we live with the denial for longer. Facades are kept up and we live in a space within ourselves trapped in from any hints of air or sunlight from greater possibilities. In the vital orientation scenario, we hit the limits of the system far more quickly and comprehensively. This is because vital orientation is driven by aggressiveness and a desire to aggrandize the sense of self. Self, however, is defined narrowly without including impacts that actions by the self have on the world and people around. This quickly brings us up against the limits of our view.

Hence, driven by the vital desire of the consumer, conspicuous consumption sets in motion disastrous ripple effects on the physical and psychological health of the people and ultimately, the health of the world. On the psychological side, people come to equate happiness and self-worth with products and "things" out there. The sense of possibility, creativeness, true as opposed to surface self-power, engendered by a worldview marked by the Fractal Ladder is all but absent. As a race, we lose subjective power and become slaves of an objective and often heartless world. The causal relationship between subjectivity and objectivity is reversed and instead of the landscape within determining the landscape without, it is the other way round. This is a poverty-stricken deal in which we have literally surrendered our source of power to a fleeting and meaningless dance towards the bottomless darkness of the abyss. Consider, for example, that in this orientation, all people are relegated to the stature of a business asset. Hence, business executives may be thought of as "more" valuable assets and may be treated more carefully. As a result, factory workers are thought of as "less" valuable assets and correspondingly treated with relatively less care, and defenseless women and children are treated as "least" valuable assets and even traded as commodities in the market.

But that is not all; the customer who is perceived as the source of money is often treated as a god—not because of any god-like qualities that may reside within them, but because they temporarily provide the lubrication for this heartless business engine to continue. If a product or service is exchanged for money, then that exchange should indicate the equality of the transaction. Yet, those who provide the service or product often continue to place the buyer on a pedestal, and the buyer himself believes that he should be placed on a pedestal. This, again, indicates the inherent and disproportionate value ascribed to money. This is a tragedy of epic proportions. The means has become the end. Yet, money is only the symbol of a force or an energy that is needed to move things in different and hopefully progressive directions. In the vaster scheme of things, it is the direction of movement in various circumstances that is of importance. In the vital scheme of things, however, it is money with its immediate power to satisfy the urge of a narrowly defined self-seeking assertiveness that is of importance.

On the tangible impacts to physical health, the stark compromise of consuming hurriedly and imperfectly thought-through products consequently replete with different sources and degrees of toxicity will take its toll on the very basis of our lives. While we have established that tobacco-based products, for instance, consumed over decades result in cancers, what we have not as meaningfully established is how a vast array of other seemingly "safe" products may similarly result in as debilitating conditions when consumed over an equal length of time. The smoke from tobacco is visible and hence more quickly has resulted in a cause–effect relationship between its consumption and ill-health. Equally debilitating toxins present in other products are however "invisible," and therefore do not as easily lend themselves to a similar cause-and-effect analyses.

The point is that given the underlying hurriedness and lack of comprehensiveness in thought and action that marks the vital orientation, it is inevitable that this vaster array of products, regardless of industry considered, will emerge as unsafe. A little more research on nutritional value in processed foods, for instance, will more broadly reveal that all enzymes are destroyed through processing and that, perhaps, a different kind of processing and distribution needs to be undergone in order to retain its nutrition value. Weston Price's *Physical Nutrition and Degeneration* (2006) stands as a classic in this area. Similarly a little more research on drug formulation may reveal, as Andrew Weil (2000) has pointed out that active ingredients in pharmaceuticals, when removed from their naturally-occurring environments and array of accompanying chemicals, have a compromising effect on cells that they come into contact with because the array and relative proportions of accompanying chemicals that existed to bring about more holistic interaction with cells has now been removed. The underlying aggression of the vital orientation does not allow for this extra time and comprehensiveness in research and development and thus of necessity must result in compromises of all sorts.

As far as negative impact on the scale of the world is concerned, we have already begun to witness the tremendous price we must pay for this orientation as evidenced by accelerated resource depletion, water and air pollution, greenhouse gas emissions, biodiversity destruction, and compromise to ecosystem services.

What we have not adequately considered, however, is the effect on global political stability. Fueled by the twin thrusts of consumer demand on the one side, which stimulates investment in new manufacturing capacity, and business desire to increase margins on the other, which stimulates outsourcing of manufacturing to "cheaper" countries, it is the "cheaper" countries that stand poised to emerge as the new global leaders as more capital flows into their regions. This is not always a good thing especially if ideology of the new global leaders is unknown or controversial or untested in the global playing field. For, it provides the country with the resources to fulfill whatever agenda may exist amongst its leadership. However, from a cause-and-effect point of view in which we must reap what we sow, the continued vital orientation at the level of individual has to create a world that is effectively vital in response. In such a world, there is little place for idealism and balanced development. There is only place for immediate fulfillment of desire to the detriment of any deeper and more holistic ideology. USA's aspiration for relative liberty, freedom, equality, and democracy, all high ideals that belong in their nature to the mental sphere, must erode when the citizens of the country are in fact not in reality practicing that, but have abandoned themselves to the petty desires and satisfactions that animate the vital sphere. If at the end of the day citizens are most concerned with bringing home a quick profit, with convenience of access to products of all kinds, and having plenty of toys to entertain themselves with, then this is the world that is going to be created. The question of how the profit is made, what the costs to the earth, people, and communities are, or what loss of self-power or ideals results, will recede into the background to be overtaken by whatever it takes to fulfill the vital-based fractal in its play across the earth.

When China arises as the world's manufacturing center to stock the inventories of the Wal-Marts of the world, people then fulfill their desires for cheaper, more easily accessible goods aimed at a portfolio of vital-level desires. That is what the seed-pattern had initiated. The seed-pattern had nothing imprinted in it about the upholding of the generative capacity of the earth, or of the peoples and communities of the earth, or of the high ideals that signal progress in the broadest sense. In its vitalistic rise, China, so it has been reported, has converted productive land into desert, polluted running and still bodies of water, compromised biodiversity, reinforced the notion that people exist for state, not only in China, but in Africa too, where it has entered into vital-level contracts with country governments. The short-sighted hunger of citizens in USA and in other rapidly growing parts of the world has fueled this rise of vitalistic dynamics and large tracts of the world are now fast becoming either centers of needless and wasteful consumption, centers of needless and wasteful manufacturing, and centers of needless and wasteful resource extraction.

The supply chains that span the world now exist to fuel this hunger and madness and in its essence, signal the organization of an inevitable destruction so long as the vital orientation persists. No amount of CSR is going to make any difference at the end of the day, unless the base consciousness of citizens the world-over, and this includes employees of companies that practice CSR and communities impacted by the operations of these companies, amongst many other stakeholder groups, completes their respective journeys through the sun-marked physical–vital–mental fractal. CSR is practised by large corporations that do not exist for CSR, but to make money. If corporations make less money, CSR programs receive less funds and CSR diminishes, unless it has become part and parcel of the way a business operates, and this can only happen if even in the absence of any calculated returns on investment, employees still practice CSR because their own fractal journeys have advanced to the mental level and they genuinely see the need for such holistic business action as represented by CSR on its own merit.

But such conversion of the world into a large supply chain, where "cheaper" countries become leaders on the world stage and more actively dictate a newer and perhaps even crasser culture for the earth, is only the beginning of the end of the vital-orientation scenario. For as resources, including the all important water, get scarcer, then a heightened irrationality will begin to dictate the politics of regions and countries and resource wars will become more prevalent. Then all manner of idealism will get dethroned as people will enter into a phase of base survival. In such a scenario, all assumptions will hopefully be questioned and the seeds for a shift to the mental level will be more powerfully bought into being.

THE LOWER MENTAL SCENARIO

In the mental-orientation scenario, questioning comes alive. This signals a significant progress, for now, all existing assumptions, many of which are of an irrational kind, can be questioned and the bases for our living consequently has a more likely chance to begin to be altered. In this scenario, raison d'être has the opportunity to come to the surface. Uniqueness and holism can begin to rise. Hence, the bases for business, amongst other modern-day institutions, can begin to be questioned, and if the questioning proceeds long enough and comprehensively enough, then more enlightened models of business and other institutions can begin to come into being.

Models in which business exists for and is accountable to a variety of stakeholders as opposed to just shareholders can come into being. Hence, business would naturally begin to alter the way in which it generates profit to begin to address all costs of its transactions on the individual, social, cultural, and environmental fronts. Similarly, other major institutions of the modern-day world can also be questioned and potentially altered to arrive at more enlightened versions of them. The often blindly-accepted tenets of religion, usually the creation of the fountainhead prophet or an ensuing circle of disciples, can be questioned and affirmed through individual self-discovery. In such a manner, the value of religion can be more truly affirmed and become more of a living force in the affairs of life. This same trajectory of questioning can then confirm the possible similarities, synergies, and complementarities of different world religions. In such a way a more enlightened institution of religion that is also a more living part of life can come into being. Education itself can be similarly questioned, and the value of spawning cogs in a pre-arranged view of life questioned, to perhaps more truly make children and youth develop along lines driven by their own natural curiosities and uniqueness.

The question of course, is at what end of the mental-orientation spectrum will all this questioning proceed at? If it proceeds at the end closer to the vital region, then in many respects, it will have the characteristic thrusts that marked the vital orientation as its accompaniment and context. Therefore, the questioning will likely not proceed comprehensively enough and what will result is a number of biased "isms" that are still anchored to the primary institution that may have characterized the recent vital milieu. Hence, even though there will be greater questioning in each of the institutions of our lives, whether of art, education, science, government, business, military, or sport, each will tend to be interpreted in terms of the recent reigning institution. In our modern-times, many will continue to interpret their value in terms of business hence. This same logic will also apply to independence and definition of countries. If USA has been perceived as being the most successful country, then its culture and driving institutions will tend to become the standard by which each country interprets its success. The degree to which McDonalds, MTV, and Levis replaces age-old institutions whether of tea drinking, *tabla*-playing, and *dhotis*, will be the measure of success of a country.

THE HIGHER MENTAL SCENARIO

At the other end of the mental-orientation spectrum, questioning will proceed more independently, and may even, at its highest, be aligned with deeper drivers that animate the intuitional level. In this scenario, each of the "isms" will tend to be truly more enlightened. Having been created through a basis of questioning though, as opposed to a deeper sense of who one is, the questioning will have its limits because it will be all about logic rather than penetrating through experience into the inner uniqueness that animates each person. When that experience becomes the center around which activity is organized, creation will proceed in a more living, organic and sustainable way. This is the essence of intuition. In the meanwhile, what will result is a number of parts of society that still function in silos or independently of each other, and not as they should, as integral parts of a single whole.

Society, hence, while objectively surfacing more of the problems that plague life, and even surfacing more of the assumptions that may have led to these problems, will still be impotent to solve them, because it has still not penetrated into the heart of Progress so long as it remains stuck in questioning without following or opening to where the questioning leads. Questioning is of course powerful, but there still needs to be a receptivity to something that is beyond the mind, for true change to happen. In the mental-orientation scenario, forms and processes may change as a result of what seems like the logical solution following the questioning. The United Nations Organization and other forms that are new and different may come into being. The extent to which they successfully achieve their missions will still remain in the balance however, so long as there are no true personalities who organize themselves not based on questioning, but on what they creatively and uniquely stand for in the scheme of things.

Hence, in this scenario, the world will likely have a burst of apparent creativity where new technology infrastructures, new types of organizations, new processes and ways of connecting people together, and new regional and global alliances at least in name, will come into being. This scenario will also result in frustration when it is discovered that all the new structures and processes and organizations have really not made the difference they intended to make. For the difference to manifest, we of necessity must enter into the intuitional orientation.

REVISITING THE INTUITIONAL SCENARIO

In the intuitional-orientation scenario, deeper questioning and completion of many sun-marked physical–vital–mental fractal journeys open one to the reality of Progress. It is in the opening to this reality that a help beyond the present-day physical, vital, and mental capabilities comes to the surface. In the disassociation from these persistent and ever-present dynamics, one becomes more of a witness to one's operations.

A freedom from the ordinary allows one to penetrate that which stands behind surfaces and the essence of what one is, in the vaster scheme of things that Progress conceivably holds in its heart, is allowed to come to the surface. In such a case, one may find what truly drives one is the essential reality of service and perfection, or adventure and courage, or knowledge and wisdom, or harmony and mutuality. In this state, if one turns one ear towards the heart of Progress, and the other towards opportunities that present themselves in the various fields of practical organization, then spontaneous, organic, living, and uniqueness-based manifestations in each of the fields of practical organization can begin to emerge.

It is then that structure and technology and process and organization will have meaning, and it is then that society will begin to work in the manner intended. When the forms one creates are expressions of who one is, there is a living and sustainable quality to them that becomes the basis for a progressive society. In this society, citizens are heroes because they have stood up for what they are at their cores and they continue to take actions that are consistent with that core. Since their cores are part of the heart of Progress, there is also a more spontaneous and integral interaction and harmony between all the various parts of society. Religion, business, art, sport, education, military, science, and country relation with country, no longer exist at loggerheads with each other. Each of the institutions remakes itself from within so that they become expressions of the deeper drivers at the heart of Progress. With true leaders at their respective helms, it is the dynamics of the Fractal Ladder and Progress itself that really guides things.

SUMMARY

These scenarios that may emerge are summarized in Figure 12.1.

FIGURE 12.1   Potential Scenarios

Physical scenario	Systemicweaknessesarecoveredup.Financialbailouts, facades,anddenialsprevail.Catastropheandupheaval looms up suddenly but surely.
Vital scenario	Frenziescontinueuntilexhaustion.Systemicdebilitation is quick. Loss of subjective power. Loss of ideals and idealism.
Lower mental scenario	Existence of biased "isms." Questioning leads to interpretation in terms of last prevailing milieu.
Higher mental scenario	Existenceofmoreenlightened"isms."Creationbasedon logic rather than on truth of uniqueness. Understanding of a lot of problems, with impotency to solve them. Burst of apparent creativity on many different fronts, followed by frustration.
Intuitional scenario	Emergence of spontaneous, organic, living, and uniqueness-basedmanifestationsacrossfields.Society works well along many different lines.

Source: Author

The question, hence, is what is to be done now. Clearly, each of the aforementioned scenarios already exist to different degrees. In the current circumstance and as the examination of many independent fractals has already revealed, it is the vital state that is most prevalent. We have just discussed the outcome of continuing to live in this state. It will result in an upheaval of calamitous proportions. We must drive towards the intuitional orientation. This means that heroes need to emerge in every walk of life. We must seize the springs of our power by disengaging from long-established norms, and in the process step onto the Fractal Ladder where our world-system begins to operate in a sustainably progressive manner. It is so that our uniqueness will come more securely to the surface, and it is so that we will each become a center for new fractals that will inevitably change the nature of organization on each rung of the Fractal Ladder and beyond. This is discussed in the next and the culminating chapter.

13

Transformation

INTRODUCTION

As a global society we operate more in the physical–vital realm than the mental–intuitional realm. The limits of the physical–vital orientation have today become abundantly clear and it is an imperative that at all levels comprising the global society we must make the shift toward a mental–intuitional orientation. To not do so is to consign ourselves to decades of needless upheaval and inevitable debilitation from the level of the individual to our very planetary system. Our very view of ourselves, corporations, and all manner of other organizations, concept of money and markets, view of other resources, view and understanding of countries and international relations, and our view of the planet and the earth–sun system, have to be re-contextualized in the light of the Progress-centered fractal system that has emerged as the possible reality of our world-system. In other words, our very worldview has to be turned on its head. There is no choice in this matter, since of necessity the very "worldview fractal" has itself to shift from the physical–vital orientation, where it has centered itself for perhaps centuries, to a mental–intuitional orientation in order to complete its own sun-marked physical–vital–mental–intuitional journey and begin to arrive at fruition. In this progressing journey, the equilibrium between objectivity and subjectivity will be reversed as internal and more subjective dynamics begin to account for more than the external and more objective dynamics. This is nothing less than a sea-change. Its time, however, has come.

In this chapter we will look at this imperative re-contextualization. There are instances of organization and pervasive dynamics where it is more immediately critical that such re-contextualization takes place. This is because these instances of organization and dynamics hold a central place in the affairs of our lives. These include the individual and her development at one end, country at the other, and commerce as the general air in-between that fills our waking and perhaps even our sleeping moments.

THE IMPERATIVE RE-CONTEXTUALIZATION

Our reality does not end with what the eye can see. This is where it begins. There is the whole informing edifice of which what the eye can see is only the final outcome. To focus only on the physical, on that which can be seen, is to focus on the surface of the edifice only, and by definition misses the causal dynamics that marks the real meaning and intent behind the physical. To focus on the physical only is to focus on established reality and to miss the reality of all the possibility that is seeking to manifest from within the heart of the edifice. And being that the heart of the edifice, the heart of Progress, is the real center around which the entire edifice and all physical manifestations revolve, to focus only on the physical, as though it were an independent reality with no connection to anything deeper, is to miss the context of life.

To imagine, therefore, that each of us are entities existing in a physical world to fulfill a part as determined by our common and most likely programmed physical–vital orientations is to consign ourselves to littleness and lack of possibility. We each become then a cog in a wheel, and depending on the randomness or luck or even effort of construction of our physical resources or vital capabilities, will play either a more or less central role in driving or moving a wheel that is headed ultimately toward its own destruction. If there is power in this, it is not power to bring about global change, but power only to accelerate debilitation of a poorly perceived and believed world-system.

Meaningful global change can come about only when the reality of one's relation with the heart of the system is rightly perceived, and by identity, the dynamics of the heart of the system begin to determine the dynamics in oneself. For this to happen, one's psychology has to go through a sea-change, and the existence of a Progress-centered, Fractal Ladder-marked, universal fractal system, of which each of us are potentially significant or insignificant fractal actors depending on if we choose to step or not to step onto the Fractal Ladder, respectively, must become a reality. In other words, a basic re-contextualizing, so that rather than experiencing ourselves as independent and isolated entities existing in the world to fulfill or aggrandize a narrow physical–vital view of ourselves by catering to dominant physical–vital dynamics abroad in each institution of life, we must begin to experience ourselves as part of the just described larger fractal system.

Such a re-contextualizing implies that we become heroes because every manner of limitation as evidenced by the pervasive and incomplete physical–vital outlook will then need to be faced, overcome, and successfully replaced by the mental–intuitional outlook that by definition begins to open us to the heart of Progress. The re-contextualizing, in fact, begins to become more real, with each stagnating or opposing fractal that we successfully overcome. In this view, we are not just cogs in a wheel, but creative centers of a continually and sustainably progressing world-system for which we are each ultimately co-responsible. There can be no more power than this.

In the face of boundary situations, and currently, as already described, we appear to be at a very significant boundary condition vis-à-vis the shift from the vital to the beginnings of the mental phase in the global economy and global society fractals, it is all the more necessary for this to be led by leadership at the individual level. The price we will pay for individuals not making the shift in their own personal fractals from a vital to a mental way of being will increase in exorbitance with every passing day.

Further, this surfacing of individual leadership must be at the core of the development of the next level of organization—be it the evolution of the business corporation or any other manner of non-profit organization. Change by arbitrary or even logically thought-out strategy or policy will never be as sustainable as change that is the result of a shift in consciousness and the consequent and organic surfacing and development of a unique personality thereby also organically re-shaping or re-making the rules of life in their own areas of influence. A person, for instance, who is able to enter into the place of creative stillness in the eye of the fractal storm, to thereby begin to approach or even to enter into the heart of Progress and from there re-make themselves, based say on some unique combination of courage, knowledge, and sense of service, will of necessity become a compelling center for the creation of a new organizational reality.

This is what must lie at the heart of the re-contextualized business or other type of organization. The usual equilibrium whereby an organization functions as a cog in the business-as-usual world must be toppled to yield to equilibrium where organization is an expression of a deeper truth that finds its roots in the very heart of Progress itself. Such an organization, if it is a business organization, will not solely exist to increase profit or market share or revenues, but to express such a deeper possibility and even to be an instrument amongst instruments tied together by the hidden orchestration of Progress, for the further development of the world-system. For is not Progress that astounding reality that has brought about shift after shift in every manner and type of fractal journey across every level of organization from the individual to the planet itself, in the face even of audacious odds?

A REDEFINED MOSAIC FOR COMMERCE

The mosaic of commerce needs to be re-contextualized. The cog-in-the-wheel, business-as-usual paradigm needs to be replaced by a business-as-expression-of-uniqueness paradigm. In the earlier stages, each business is a field for individuals to express their truer individualities. It is a field for truer creativity in which core dynamics, such as the sense of curiosity and adventure, the unbiased pursuit of knowledge, the remaking of every manner of harmony— from the harmony between people in the organization, between business process and external environment and society, between business and business takes place as the natural expression of the business, and the sense of service and perfection in all that is done is done for the sake of service and perfection and not because one becomes richer or more famous in the bargain. But this cannot happen through checklists and processes and installed technologies, though these may, at certain points, provide a helping hand. It has to happen because that true sense of curiosity, courage, and adventure, or of an unbiased pursuit of and openness to knowledge, or of the need for creating ever more solid and uniting harmonies based perhaps on recognition and appreciation of difference, or of the need of serving and doing every minute task with a sense of absolute perfection and even as an offering incarnates in the being of individuals, who by force and authenticity of those incarnations become the natural leaders in the circumstance. At the more mature stages, each business is a note in a fantastic score orchestrated by Progress to bring about true, un-end-able, sustainable progress at each level of creation—from the individual, to the team and larger collectivity, to the environment, and to society itself.

But for all this to take place, the notion that business exists to make money must be toppled on its head. The color and frontal pervasiveness of money has pauperized the mosaic of commerce. Instead of the potential richness of unique threads interweaving as per imagination of beauty, there is a standardizing face that appears in every nook and corner of the mosaic. The true sense of courage and adventure, pursuit of knowledge, building of harmonies, and service and perfection, has been re-imaged by a common red and any sense of surfacing uniqueness has been easily drowned in the vast standardizing sea. In today's world, without money one cannot live. All worth is measured by money. All progress is estimated by some variation of monetary indicators. Many organizations state their purpose in terms of making money. The only viable currency is money-based. In its reality, such an orientation marks an anchoring in the vital consciousness. Acquisition of money allows immediate satisfaction of desire and a sense of power. But as with all stances that emanate from the vital consciousness, this orientation is markedly short-sighted and reinforces our lives as prisoners of the past. The sense of money must be re-contextualized by a completion of its own fractal, and restated in terms of a mental–intuitional orientation.

In the mental–intuitional orientation, the context of life is shifted from one of separate and isolated entities seeking for their own narrow fulfillment in whatever way possible, to one of a single all-containing, all-present, all-informing system expressing itself in apparent islands of uniqueness, that give the system its true meaning by fully becoming the unique entity that marks it from every other island also expressing its unique uniqueness.

In such a view, money too is seen as fundamentally different. In the physical–vital orientation, its value is in its accumulation since this allows the accumulating entity to fulfill the continually arising physical and vital needs that marks humanity at that level. Worth naturally is measured in terms of money since it is its amassed power that allows the physical–vital entity to fulfill desire through the disbursement of it. In the mental–intuitional view, its value is in allowing the many facets of progress, expressed by uniqueness and differentiation from the level of the person to corporations and organizations of all kinds, to continue to develop. The focus is on the expression of unique and differentiated authenticity in all fields and at all levels of life. Money is the lubricator, the stimulator, the force, that currently facilitates that development to take place. In the mental–intuitional view the emphasis is on authentic facets of progress.

If it is this that is pursued, then money will be drawn to that as iron filings are drawn to a magnet. Worth is not measured in terms of money that has accumulated, but in terms of new paths that have been hewn in the adventure of life, new knowledge that has been discovered, greater harmonies that have been established, or in more detailed contours of service and perfection that may have emerged. The audacity of a story, the peace in the atmosphere around one who has experienced the vastness and pervasiveness of the system, the compelling smile on a face, the intricacy of perfection in a dance, may themselves be the currency of exchange that binds and inspires people and efforts to continue to develop. These currencies, for a while, may be interchangeable with money, as today the Dollar is with the Yen, but as the Fractal of Exchange tends more and more towards the intuitional will of them become the whole means by which development is instigated and continued. Money is an interim measure. It is a symbol for an energy required to move things around. There was barter of goods with focus on the good themselves at the "physical" level of commerce, there is exchange of money with an increasing and even outright de-linking to all notions of goods at the "vital" level, there will be a broader system of exchange encompassing monetary and non-monetary instruments such as smiles and displays of knowledge re-linked to a vaster spectrum of goods at the "mental" level, and finally an exchange of consciousness as we tend towards the "intuitional" levels. This journey of exchange, of which money is a part, is summarized in Figure 13.1.

FIGURE 13.1 The Exchange Fractal

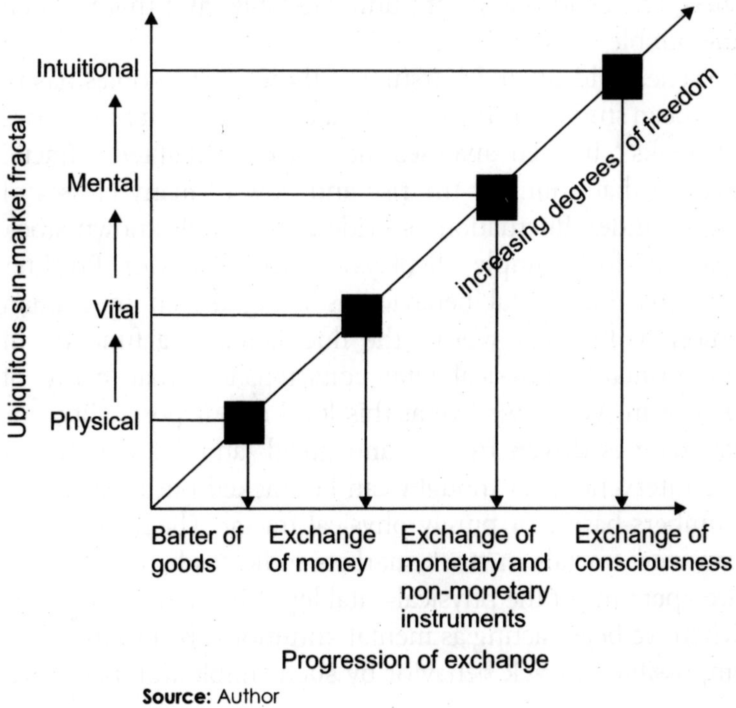

Source: Author

The focus on accumulation and often irrational accumulation of money, rather than on the potential uses of money, has caused the recent global financial crises. Biased or even blind accumulation of money by primarily physical–vital entities, be they individuals, banks, or other investment mechanisms, has led to the increasing de-linking of money with real development. Hence, an array of asset bubbles where the value of an asset in question, be it technology stocks to real estate on the more concrete side, and far more difficult to understand and track derivatives and similar financial instruments on the less concrete side, is continually increased as it is traded by individuals and organizations hungry to accumulate more wealth, and the increase in the bubble itself comes to be seen as the point of the value. Somewhere along the line, it is realized that these castles in the air are uninhabitable, and this is when the bubble bursts.

The build-up and bursting of these asset bubbles has in fact been studied by the likes of Elliott and Prechter in a series of books.[1] In their analyses they have highlighted a fractal pattern that animates the rise and flow of many classes of assets. Index fluctuation as evidenced in well-known stock markets, for example, displays a fractal behavior. Prechter explains this fractal behavior as being driven by human emotion. In other words, the fluctuation is a function of the primarily physical–vital consciousness that many of us live in. When we live at this level of our possibility, our behavior is driven by fear and greed, and the absence of the intervention of thought can be tracked out by a simple numbers-based, or purely physical fractal. The fact that we can view fractals in stock markets indicates hence, that we are operating at the physical–vital level. It is to be noted that when we begin acting as mental–intuitional beings it will be impossible to track behavior by such simple number-based one-dimensional fractals. Asset rising and bursting of the nature that has caused the recent global financial crises will be impossible to occur.

Similarly, the notion that growth of economies, locally, regionally, and internationally has to proceed along a trajectory of increasing GDP or GNP or however economic growth may be tracked has caused a lot of consternation. But why should there not be a cycle to growth where increase alternates with decrease? Why should savings rates of individuals and hence choice not to consume in certain years not increase at will? Why should periods of liquidity availability not alternate with a liquidity crunch? The point is that the orientation that the flow of goods and services and money has to increase from year-to-year regardless of the way it impacts progress, a vital orientation, in order that our existence as a species is justified is flawed. Night alternates with day and assimilation, integration, and silence are as important to long-term and integral growth as periods of heightened activity. If the focus of attention was fixed on the underlying progress rather than on the flow of money that in reality can at best lubricate potential progress, we would be much better of in even tackling fiscal and monetary policies. This cannot happen, though, unless we begin to anchor ourselves in the mental–intuitional orientation.

Our current perception of money is a great binding chain. It has bound the individual to a life of triviality as even basic needs have become linked to accumulation of money. It has also bound the large majority of organizations, from the business to many other types, to equating all activity and resource-base, not to mention output of the organization in monetary terms. Again, it has bound society to track its own development in terms of the crudities of GNP and GDP.[2] But, as mentioned earlier, it is only the person who is close to death who may worry about their intake of oxygen. In the mental–intuitional view, the system is perceived as one system with Progress at the center. In this view, just as oxygen does not belong to anyone money really belongs to no one. It is a facilitator of activity. When one begins to live in a space in alignment with the heart of Progress, our hypothesis, following the scaling of a conscious system seeding its own development, is that money flows to support the ensuing activity. The activity, as opposed to the money, may therefore more accurately belong to a person. Progress, hence, needs to be measured in terms of activity. This, really, would be progress.

To live in the physical–vital orientation and expect money to be free is a chimera. The physical–vital orientation is one of severe limitation because its actors cannot see beyond the end of their noses. Even though our vast earth-sun system possesses an abundance of water and energy, and hope and love and knowledge, for instance, a narrow view will never open the actors to these possibilities of infinity. When hardwork has been done, however, and many fractal journeys at many instances and levels have successfully been completed, then the fire of Progress will be concretely felt where perhaps it is now subtly hiding or covered in circumstance. Then, as actors enter into the mental–intuitional orientation and begin to enter into the heart of Progress, and feel the incarnation of uniqueness amidst the vast and unifying system, the outlook will shift to one of possibility and abundance, and then money will become free. It is then that the overwhelming red will recede into the background, perhaps only to be depicted by traces and bypaths to indicate its flow, and the other diverse threads patterning out new colors and possibilities will come into relief in a re-contextualized mosaic of commerce.

The contrasting attitudes towards money are summarized in Figure 13.2.

FIGURE 13.2   Perspectives on Money

Physical–vital	Mental–intuitional
Value of money in accumulation	Money as a lubricator that facilitates diverse development
Worth measured in terms of money	Worth measured in terms of new paths, new knowledge, greater harmony, more detailed perfection and service
Money exchanged with money	Money exchanged with other non-monetary instruments, including consciousness
De-linking of money with real development, leading to array of asset bubbles	Focus on activity and development as measure of success
Necessity of continued growth whether measured by GNP, consumption, etc.	Conscious system seeds its own development through appropriate flows of money
Money as a great binding chain at individual, corporate, societal levels	Money as oxygen Money as belonging to no one
Money as potentially very expensive	Money as inexpensive since it automatically flows to most appropriate venture
Blind to true abundance	Awareness and openness to abundance
Asset bubbles rising and bursting a function of simple number-based fractals	Asset bubble rising and bursting cannot occur

Source: Author

MULTIPLICATION OF MOSAICS

Such freedom will allow society to be redefined along multiple paths of development, and all manner of unique and breathtaking organizations, collectivities, communities, and cultures will come into existence by dint of the separate and interacting lines of development. For the binding chain that currently blinds societal institutions will have been severed and the creative possibilities inherent in the heart of Progress will find more unbiased expression. A mosaic, like the mosaic of commerce, will also exist for every other institution in society. Hence, with one institutional mosaic combined with every other, what will result is an intricate, detailed, beautiful, harmonious, bold, and varied expression and reality of possibility. Each of these collectivities will be driven by unique individualities who have begun to gain mastery over the fractal vortex that surrounds their lives by stepping onto the Fractal Ladder and consequently entering into relationship with Progress.

The notion that countries have to follow a standard trajectory of development will also become defunct. This has been the emphasis in recent decades and, not surprisingly, since we have traversed the vital phase where dynamics of selfish aggrandizement trump all other dynamics. In the vital phase, life is understood and seen as a play of a few key developments of this nature. Fukuyama (1993), argues that the advent of Western liberal democracy may signal the end-point of humanity's socio-cultural evolution and the final form of human government. A worldview of this nature is consistent with such a physical–vital orientation. In the mental–intuitional phase, the mosaic of development alters and countries express what they are in their essence rather than what the urge to amass surface and short-sighted wealth may cause them to become. The deeper identity and formative forces that by definition cannot be random since they have been likely orchestrated by the play of Progress through the instrumentation of prior fractal leaders at the individual and organizational levels can have a chance to be more clearly understood and come more actively to the surface.

As in the development of uniqueness at the individual level, where the play of four characteristics or tendencies may determine true individuality, so too in understanding the essence of country culture, the four characteristics are likely to shed light. India, for example, can be thought of in terms of penetrating into the depths of knowledge and harmonizing all of life around that knowledge. England, on the other hand, is perhaps about harmonizing life around a very practical and world-wisely knowledge. Japan, it may be said, is about incarnating the spirit of courage and nobility and coupling that with a deep and harmonious aestheticism. Similarly, every other country has some deep drivers at its core that have been responsible for creating the essence of its culture. In the vital phase that we are now in process of completing, these deeper possibilities though present in exceptional individuals and organizations, have largely been covered up or marginalized because of the excessive focus on surface dynamics. Entry into the mental–intuitional levels will allow these deeper and formative dynamics to come into relief. Then the essence of the culture will be strengthened and made more diverse and varied in its essential and unique unity.

In this view, every country, through process of its history, has developed a unique culture that must be cherished and must become part of the basis by which each country not only further develops its own possibilities, but also influences how parts of the world relate to and learn from other parts of the world. There is no developed culture, regardless of size, that is not worthy of existing. Its coming into existence in the face of baffling odds stacked to maintain the status quo is sign enough that the hand of Progress has itself likely pushed something of its possibility to the surface for manifestation. International relations, now, often an outcome of political calculation and a move to strengthen a country's influence or own stability even if through exploitation of other parts of the world, has also to be toppled to become an exchange of living cultures and mutual learning. Otherwise, why else would all manner of uniqueness manifest in the earth-play if not to not only express possibility from the heart of Progress and encourage through example of uniqueness and way of being the similar development of that very strain of possibility in other entities, but also to create a richly profound diversity that becomes the basis of true and everlasting progress and sustainability.

SUMMARY

This then is the immediate transformation that needs to take place at the levels of the individual, the organization, the country, and with society. All this transformation has, as its basis, the shift of consciousness of the individual, and it is imperative that we provide the space and basis for this transformation to take place. On it hangs the development of every other level of practical creation and our reinforced play on the Fractal Ladder. It is only so that all present conundrums can be transcended and it is only so that we can most safely usher in the future incarnations of Progress.

Notes

CHAPTER 1

1. Refer to Brigg (1992) and Gleick (1988) as starters in this subject.
2. The terms physical, vital, mental were coined by Sri Aurobindo. Refer to *Sri Aurobindo's Collected Works*, Sri Aurobindo Ashram.

CHAPTER 4

1. See Balkan (2005) for a more detailed examination of this subject.
2. See Brittain-Catlin (2006) for a more detailed treatment of this subject.

CHAPTER 5

1. Refer to Colin (2004) for further discussion on this.
2. Refer to Benyus (2002) for a more elaborate treatment of this subject.

CHAPTER 6

1. Please note that while the creation of these phases is only a thought experiment applying the emerging fractal model, Sri Aurobindo's *The Life Divine* (published by Sri Aurobindo Ashram), has the most detailed and robust explanations of evolution I have been exposed to. This thought experiment is likely influenced by his thought.
2. Refer to Don Tapscott (1996) for a more detailed treatment of this subject.
3. Refer to James Lovelock (2006) for a detailed treatment of the Gaia hypothesis.

CHAPTER 9

1. In Sri Aurobindo's *The Mother* (published by Sri Aurobindo Ashram), Sri Aurobindo describes four active powers: *maheshwari* (knowledge), *mahakali* (power), *mahalakshmi* (harmony), and *mahasaraswati* (service and perfection) that govern manifested existence. These four terms arrived at here have similarities with these four powers.
2. Refer to Sri Aurobindo's *The Upanishads* (1981) which has a translation of portions of the Mandukya Upanishad relating to AUM.

CHAPTER 10

1. There are many books on climate change. See Flannery (2001) for a deeper treatment of climate change.
2. For an overview of CSR, refer to John Elkington (1999).
3. Refer to Becker and Selden (1998) for a more detailed treatment of this subject.
4. For a detailed illustration of how the oil and gas and the automobile industries have compromised our lives, see Tamminen (2008).
5. Refer to Jared Diamond (2005) for an illustration of the instability of a narrow one-dimensional societal focus.

CHAPTER 13

1. We made reference to "The Elliott Wave Principle" in Chapter 1. Also refer to Prechter (2002).
2. See Talberth (2008) for alternatives to GDP/GNP.

References

Balkan, Joe. 2005. *The Corporation: The Pathological Pursuit of Profit and Power*. New York, USA: Free Press.

Becker, Robert and Gary Selden. 1998. *The Body Electric: Electromagnetism and the Foundation of Life*. New York, USA: Harper Paperbacks.

Benyus, Janine. 2002. *Biomimicry: Innovation Inspired by Nature*. New York, USA: Harper-Perennial.

Brigg, John. 1992. *Fractals: The Patterns of Chaos*. New York, USA: Simon & Schuster.

Brittain-Catlin, William. 2006. *Offshore: The Dark Side of the Global Economy*. New York, USA: Picador.

Colin, Campbell. 2004. *The Coming Oil Crisis*. Essex, UK: Multi-Science Publishing.

Diamond, Jared. 2005. *Collapse: How Societies Choose to Fail or Succeed*. New York, USA: Penguin.

Elkington, John. 1999. *Cannibals with Forks: Triple Bottom Line of 21st Century Business*. Oxford, UK: Capstone Publishing Ltd.

Flannery, Tim. 2001. *The Weather Makers: How Man is Changing the Climate and what it Means for Life on Earth*. New York, USA: Grove Press.

Fukuyama, Francis. 1993. *The End of History and the Last Man*. New York, USA: Harper Perennial.

Fuller, Buckmister. 1982. *Synergetics: Explorations in the Geometry of Thinking*. New York, USA: Macmillan.

Frost, A.J. and R.R. Prechter. 2001. *Elliott Wave Principle: Key to Market Behavior*. Gainesville, USA: Wiley.

Gleick, James. 1988. *Chaos: Making a New Science*. New York, USA: Penguin.

Lovelock, James. 2006. *The Revenge of Gaia*. New York, USA: Basic Books.

Mandelbrot, Benoît B. 1982. *The Fractal Geometry of Nature*. New York, USA: W.H. Freeman and Co.

Mandelbrot, Benoît and Richard L. Hudson. 2004. *The (Mis)Behavior of Markets: A Fractal View of Risk, Ruin, and Reward*. New York, USA: Basic Books.

Maslow, A.H. 1943. "A Theory of Human Motivation," *Psychological Review*, 50(4): 370–96.

McDonough, William and Michael Braungart. 2002. *Cradle to Cradle: Remaking the Way We Make Things*. New York, USA: North Point Press.

Perkins, John. 2005. *Confessions of an Economic Hit Man*. San Francisco, USA: Berret-Koehler Publishers.

Prechter, Robert R. 2002. *Conquer the Crash*. Chichester, UK: New Classics Library.

Price, Weston. 2006. *Physical Nutrition and Degeneration*, 6th Edition. Canaan, USA: Keats Pub.

Seagal, Sandra and David Horne. 1997. *Human Dynamics*. Waltham, MA, USA: Pegasus Communications.

Sri Aurobindo. 1950–51. *Savitri*, First Edition. Pondicherry, India: Sri Aurobindo Ashram Press.

————. 1981. *The Upanishads*. Pondicherry, India: Sri Aurobindo Ashram.

Talberth, John. 2008. "A New Bottom Line for Progress," in The WorldWatch Institute's *2008 State of the World: Toward a Sustainable Economy*, pp. 18–31. New York, USA: W.W. Norton & Company.

Tamminen, Terry. 2008. *Lives per Gallon: The True Cost of our Oil Addiction*. Washington DC, USA: Shearwater.

Tapscott, Don. 1996. *The Digital Economy*. New York, USA: McGraw-Hill Book Company.

Weil, Andrew. 2000. *Spontaneous Healing: How to Discover and Embrace Your Body's Natural Ability to Maintain and Heal Itself*. New York, USA: Ballantine Books.

About the Author

Pravir Malik is the founder and president of Aurosoorya—
an organization focused on fractal systems architecture.
He has been the Managing Director at Business for Social
Responsibility (BSR) and has also been a founding member
of A.T. Kearney India. Pravir Malik is a change architect
who draws insight into potential futures through a study
of global trends and patterns, systems theory and human
potential. Most of his work in the last two decades has been
focused on the corporate sector, helping leaders in large
organizations bring about significant organizational and
business changes.

He has written two books on the future of organizations:
India's Contribution to Management (2000) and *Flowering of
Management* (1997).

About the Author